MW00680428

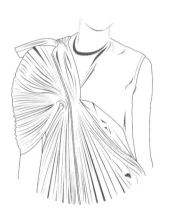

© 2014 **booq** publishing, S.L.
c/ València, 93, Pral. 1ª
08029 Barcelona, Spain

Editorial coordinator:
Claudia Martínez Alonso

Art director:
Mireia Casanovas Soley

Layout:
Guillermo Pfaff Puigmartí
Sara Abril

Translation:
Cillero & de Motta

ISBN 978-84-942639-4-1

Printed in Spain

6   A SMALL DETAIL MAKES A BIG DIFFERENCE
    KLEINES DETAIL – GROSSER UNTERSCHIED
    UN PEQUEÑO DETALLE MARCA LA GRAN DIFERENCIA

8   COLLARS AND NECKLINES
    KRÄGEN UND AUSSCHNITTE
    CUELLOS Y ESCOTES

70 SHOULDERS AND SLEEVES
    SCHULTERN UND ÄRMEL
    HOMBROS Y MANGAS

116 WAISTLINES
    TAILLEN
    CINTURAS

140 POCKETS, ZIPPERS AND BUTTONS
    TASCHEN, REISSVERSCHLÜSSE UND KNÖPFE
    BOLSILLOS, CIERRES Y BOTONES

170 GATHERING AND DRAPING
    FALTEN, KNITTER UND RAFFUNGEN
    FRUNCIDOS Y DRAPEADOS

198 PLEATS AND FLOUNCES
    PLISSEES, RÜSCHEN UND BESÄTZE
    PLISADOS Y VOLANTES

220 DECORATIVE APPLIQUÉS
    DEKORATIVE APPLIKATIONEN
    APLICACIONES DECORATIVAS

248 SEWING DETAILS
    DETAILS BEI NÄHTEN UND SÄUMEN
    DETALLES DE COSTURA

274 BIOGRAPHIES
    BIOGRAPHIES
    REFERENCIAS BIOGRÁFICAS

A SMALL DETAIL MAKES A BIG DIFFERENCE

The saying that small details make a big difference is certainly not new, we are all aware of the significance. In fact, in any differential marketing strategy, a product is special and different from the rest of the market for those details that makes it unique. In fashion, the same rules apply. Proof of this are those details that are now trademarks for many fashion houses such as the Chanel neckline by the French designer, which Karl Lagerfeld has reinvented year after year, the flounces patented by the prestigious Spanish designers Victorio & Lucchino that they call "caracola". Or details that have become icons of an era, such as the Gaultier's cone-shaped corset created for Madonna's Blond Ambition Tour, which was an emblematic symbol of fashion in the early nineties.

The history of costume shows us the important role that details have played in fashion over the years. For centuries, they have defined the distinctive features of each period and the differentiation between social classes and groups. Each moment has contributed new elements that represent an infinite source of inspiration for designers all over the world. The magic of fashion is its consistent ability to evolve, combining new materials with more traditional materials, inventing and reviving past fashions. It is not an easy task to reinterpret elements from other times and cultures, however, with careful research, many designers have been captivated by past practices and have managed to reinterpret them. Details from former times are constantly reappearing on international runways such as the Baroque Medici collar, the Renaissance ruffled sleeves and other types from far-off places, made with techniques such as Japanese origami or embroidery with designation of origin, such as Ñandutí lace, traditional Paraguayan, or French knots.

In this book we will visit Fashion Weeks in New York, Paris, Milan, London, Madrid, Copenhagen, Berlin, Mexico, Lisbon, Moscow, Tokyo and so on, with collections featuring both classic and more revolutionary styles, through which we will show international trends and the most eye-catching details in current fashion. Designers such as Manish Arora, Maison Martin Margiela, Tsumori Chisato and Kris Van Assche together with the major names in fashion and new hopes from first class design schools that bring an air of freshness to this project. In these times of imminent globalization, the fashion industry researches and becomes immersed in the pursuit for ethnic and cultural values salvaged from remote civilizations. For this reason, we have included a selection of designers from over twenty different countries; whose designs and the care with which the details are made are an example of the cultural richness that we have yet to discover and the contribution that intercultural exchange can offer a market such as the fashion industry.

A universe of details categorized into eight chapters that invite you to take a fresh look at the world of fashion and its endless possibilities.

KLEINES DETAIL – GROSSER UNTERSCHIED

Dass kleine Details einen großen Unterschied ausmachen, ist ja nichts Neues, denn wir alle sind uns ihrer Bedeutung bewusst. Tatsächlich beruht jede differenzierte Marketingstrategie darauf, dass ein Produkt dann etwas Besonderes wird, wenn es sich durch einzigartige Details von den anderen Produkten am Markt unterscheidet. In der Mode gilt das Gleiche. Ein Beleg hierfür sind die besonderen Einzelheiten, die als unverwechselbares Markenzeichen eines Modeunternehmens gelten, wie z. B der typische Kragen von Chanel, der von der französischen Designerin entwickelt wurde und den Karl Lagerfeld Jahr für Jahr neu erfand; die verspielten Rüschen und Volants der spanischen Designer Victorio & Lucchino oder die Entwürfe, die als Ikonen einer bestimmten Epoche gelten – wie die Bodys mit spitzen Kegeln, die Gaultier für Madonnas Blond Ambition Tour entwarf und die als Symbol der Mode des Anfangs der neunziger Jahre gelten.

Die Geschichte der Bekleidung zeigt, welche Bedeutung den Details in der Mode über die Epochen hinweg zukam. Seit Jahrhunderten kennzeichnen sie die einzigartigen Merkmale eine jeden Zeitalters sowie die Unterschiede zwischen einzelnen Gesellschaftsklassen und sozialen Gruppen. Die Mode hat im Verlauf der Zeit immer neue Elemente beigetragen, die heute als unerschöpfliche Quelle der Inspiration für Designer weltweit dienen. Die Magie der Mode liegt in ihrer konstanten Fähigkeit, sich zu einwickeln, neue Materialien mit traditionelleren Stoffen zu verbinden und Trends, die längst aus der Mode sind, neu zu erfinden und wiederzubeleben. Die Interpretation der Elemente aus anderen Zeiten oder Kulturen ist nicht einfach, infolge gründlicher Forschungsarbeit begeisterten sich viele Designer für die Arbeiten vergangener Zeiten und fanden einen Weg, sie für die heutige Zeit neu zu interpretieren. Auf den internationalen Laufstegen sehen wir Details aus vergangenen Zeiten mit neuem Leben erfüllt, darunter der Stuartkragen des Barock, die Schinkenärmel der Renaissance und andere Elemente aus fernen Zeiten, gefertigt mit Techniken wie dem japanischen Origami oder Stickereien unterschiedlichster Herkunft, darunter die traditionell paraguayische Ñandutí oder der französische Knötchenstich.

In diesem Buch nehmen wir eine detaillierte Analyse der Modewochen in New York, Paris, Mailand, London, Madrid, Kopenhagen, Berlin, Mexiko, Lissabon, Moskau, Tokio und vielen anderen Städten vor und sehen uns an, was dort gezeigt wird – von streng klassischen bis hin zu überschäumend revolutionären Entwürfen und präsentieren damit die internationalen Trends und die spektakulärsten Details der aktuellen Mode. Designer wie Manish Arora, Maison Martin Margiela, Tsumori Chisato oder Kris Van Assche werden ebenso gezeigt wie die großen Talente der Mode und neue, aufgehende Sterne aus hervorragenden Designschulen, die diesem Projekt frischen Wind verleihen. In diesen Zeiten der Globalisierung leistet die Mode Forschungsarbeit und begibt sich auf die Suche nach ethnischen und kulturellen Werten, die von den im Verborgenen lebenden Zivilisationen ins Heute gerettet wurden. Aus diesem Grund stellen wir eine Auswahl an Designern aus über zwanzig verschiedenen Nationen vor, deren Liebe zum Detail Zeugnis des kulturellen Reichtums ist, den es noch zu entdecken gilt und die zeigt, welchen Beitrag die Interkulturalität zu einem Markt wie dem der Mode leisten kann.

Ein Universum aus Einzelheiten, klassifiziert und geordnet in acht Kapitel, laden Sie ein, die Welt der Mode mit neuen Augen und dem Bewusstsein für die grenzenlosen Möglichkeiten der Kreativität zu entdecken.

UN PEQUEÑO DETALLE MARCA LA GRAN DIFERENCIA

Que los pequeños detalles marcan la diferencia no es ninguna novedad, puesto que todos somos conscientes de la importancia que tienen. De hecho, en cualquier estrategia diferencial de marketing, un producto se convierte en especial y diferente al del resto del mercado por aquellos detalles que hacen de él algo único. En la moda ocurre exactamente lo mismo. Muestra de ello son los que han servido como sello de muchas firmas de moda, como el cuello Chanel que lanzó la diseñadora francesa y que Karl Lagerfeld ha reinventado año tras año, los volantes caracola patentados por los prestigiosos diseñadores españoles Victorio & Lucchino, o aquellos que se han convertido en iconos de una época, como las copas en forma de cono que remataban el corsé que Gaultier creó para el *Blond Ambition Tour* de Madonna y que fue todo un emblema de la moda de principios de los años noventa.

La historia del traje nos muestra la importancia que han tenido los detalles en la moda a través de los tiempos. Durante siglos, han marcado los rasgos distintivos de cada periodo y la diferenciación entre clases y grupos sociales. Cada momento ha aportado nuevos elementos que hoy representan una inagotable fuente de inspiración para diseñadores de todo el mundo. La magia de la moda es su capacidad constante de evolucionar, de combinar nuevos materiales con los más tradicionales, de inventar y de revivir modas ya sobrevenidas. No es fácil reinterpretar elementos de otros tiempos o culturas; sin embargo, con un meticuloso trabajo de investigación, muchos diseñadores han caído prendidos de labores antiguas y han sabido reinterpretarlas. En las pasarelas internacionales veremos como aparecen detalles de tiempos pasados como el cuello Médicis del Barroco, las mangas jamón del Renacimiento y otros de procedencia lejana, construidos con técnicas como el origami japonés o los bordados con denominación de origen, tan dispares como el encaje ñandutí, de tradición paraguaya, o el punto de nudo francés.

En este libro haremos un extenso recorrido por las semanas de la moda de Nueva York, París, Milán, Londres, Madrid, Copenhague, Berlín, México, Lisboa, Moscú, Tokio y un largo etcétera, con propuestas que van desde prendas clásicas hasta las más revolucionarias, con las que mostraremos las tendencias internacionales y los detalles más espectaculares de la moda actual. Diseñadores de la talla de Manish Arora, Maison Martin Margiela, Tsumori Chisato o Kris Van Assche conviven con grandes talentos de la moda y nuevas promesas de excelentes escuelas de diseño que aportan frescura a este proyecto. En estos tiempos en los que acecha la globalización, la moda investiga y se sumerge en la búsqueda de valores étnicos y culturales rescatados de civilizaciones recónditas. Por este motivo, incluimos una selección de diseñadores de más de veinte nacionalidades distintas, cuyos diseños y el mimo con que elaboran los detalles son una muestra de la riqueza cultural que aún nos queda por descubrir y del aporte que la interculturalidad proporciona a un mercado como el de la moda.

Un universo de detalles clasificados y organizados en ocho capítulos que te invita a descubrir el mundo de la moda con nuevos ojos y un sinfín de posibilidades.

COLLARS AND NECKLINES

KRÄGEN UND AUSSCHNITTE

CUELLOS Y ESCOTES

A garment's neckline or collar can be the secret weapon to turn a simple garment into a sublime garment, which also gives the wearer one personality or another: casual, sensual, romantic or elegant. Many of them are revived and changed according to the era. A perfect example is the halterneck, which was a runaway success for evening gowns in the thirties; then it became popular in the seventies by labels such as Halston, and at the start of this century it regained strength again. This chapter offers an extensive selection of collars and necklines used in the latest international collections. We will take a look at well-defined models, which in themselves are the key to the whole outfit, and others that are complemented with appliqués and accessories that make the outfit stand out. They are all here, from the classic round necks, V-necks, crew necks and turtlenecks, to boat necks, mao necks, asymmetrical, strapless etc. Endless interpretations of necklines and elaborate designs that convert collars into works of art, architectural pieces or divine jewels.

Der zu einem Kleidungsstück entworfene Ausschnitt oder Kragen kann das Geheimnis sein, das ein einfaches in ein edles Teil verwandelt und gleichzeitig der Trägerin oder dem Träger eine bestimmte Persönlichkeit verleiht: lässig, sinnlich, romantisch oder elegant. Viele von ihnen werden aus früheren Epochen wieder aufgegriffen und zeitgemäß modifiziert. Ein deutliches Beispiel ist der Halter-Ausschnitt, der in den dreißiger Jahren an Abendkleidern sehr beliebt war, in den Siebzigern dank Marken wie Halston erneut wertgeschätzt wurde und zu Beginn dieses Jahrhunderts wieder an Bedeutung gewinnt. Dieses Kapitel umfasst eine breite Auswahl an Krägen und Ausschnitten, die in den letzten internationalen Entwürfen enthalten waren. Wir sehen recht definierte Modelle, die sich selbst genügen, und andere, die um verfeinernde und raffinierte Applikationen oder Accessoires ergänzt wurden. Die großen Klassiker sind vertreten: Rund-, V-, Kastenausschnitt, Rollkragen; Matrosen-, Mao-, asymmetrischer Kragen, Korsett, & Eine Unzahl an Interpretationen dieser sehr edlen Ausschnitte und Designs, die Krägen in göttliche Kunstwerke, Architektur oder Schmuckstücke verwandeln.

El escote o cuello que se diseña para una prenda puede ser el secreto que transforme una pieza sencilla en una sublime y que, a su vez, otorgue una u otra personalidad a quien finalmente la vista: desenfadada, sensual, romántica o elegante. Muchos de ellos resurgen y se modifican según la época. Un claro ejemplo es el escote *halter*, que tuvo un gran éxito en los vestidos de noche de los años treinta, se revalorizó en los setenta gracias a firmas como Halston y a principios de este siglo volvió a tomar fuerza. En este capítulo se recoge una amplia selección de cuellos y escotes presentes en las últimas propuestas internacionales. Veremos modelos bastante definidos, que por sí mismos aportan la clave al conjunto, y otros que se complementan con aplicaciones o accesorios que lo potencian y realzan. Están representados los grandes clásicos, los cuellos redondos, en V, a la caja, cisne; los cuellos barca, mao, asimétricos, palabra de honor... Un sinfín de interpretaciones de estos escotes y diseños muy elaborados que convierten los cuellos en obras de arte, piezas arquitectónicas o joyas divinas.

AMERICAN PÉREZ
SPAIN

001

002

THE SWEDISH SCHOOL OF TEXTILES
SWEDEN

ANJARA
SPAIN

003

004

ANJARA
SPAIN

THE SWEDISH SCHOOL OF TEXTILES
SWEDEN

005

006

AMERICAN PÉREZ
SPAIN

BORA AKSU
TURKEY

007

008

VICTORIO & LUCCHINO
SPAIN

ELISA PALOMINO
SPAIN

009

010

TSUMORI CHISATO
JAPAN

BEBA'S CLOSET
SPAIN

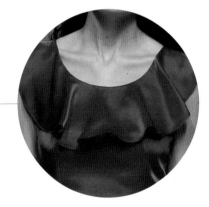

011

012

MANISH ARORA
INDIA

ANA LOCKING
SPAIN

013

014

MANISH ARORA
INDIA

TSUMORI CHISATO
JAPAN

015

016

DIMITRI
ITALY

13

MANISH ARORA

INDIA

017

018

ANA LOCKING

SPAIN

THE SWEDISH SCHOOL OF TEXTILES

SWEDEN

019

020

LEMONIEZ

SPAIN

CATI SERRÀ
SPAIN

021

022

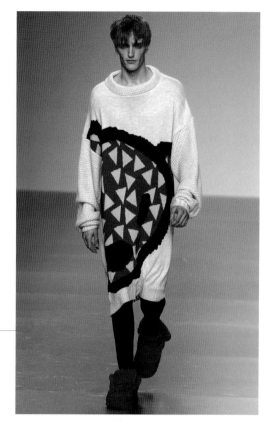

MARTA MONTOTO
SPAIN

CATI SERRÀ
SPAIN

023

024

MALINI RAMANI
USA/INDIA

BIBIAN BLUE
SPAIN

025

026

THE SWEDISH SCHOOL OF TEXTILES
SWEDEN

DIMITRI
ITALY

027

028

BOHENTO
SPAIN

MALINI RAMANI

USA/INDIA

029

030

ALI CHARISMA

INDONESIA

BOHENTO

SPAIN

031

032

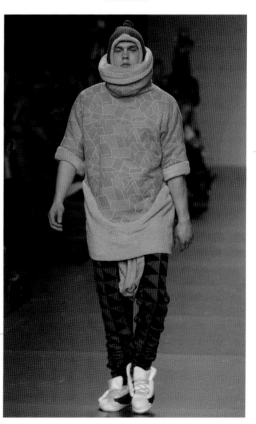

MARTA MONTOTO

SPAIN

THE SWEDISH SCHOOL OF TEXTILES
SWEDEN

033

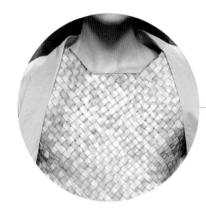

034

MARTIN LAMOTHE
SPAIN

CHARLIE LE MINDU
FRANCE

035

036

AILANTO
SPAIN

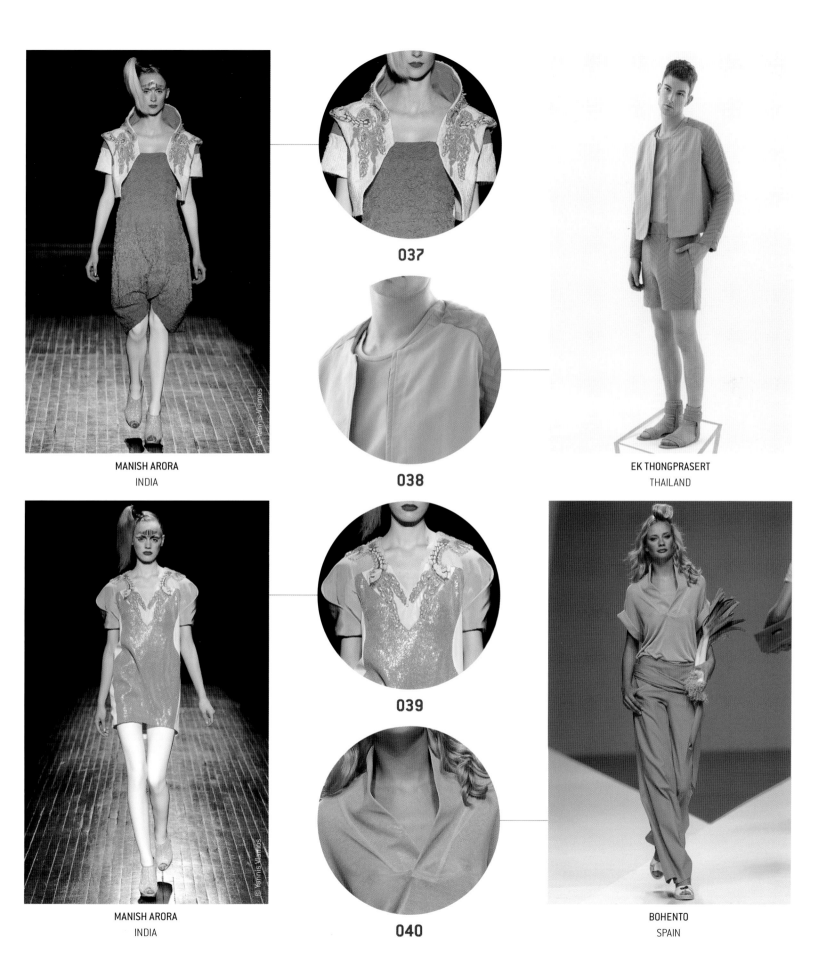

MANISH ARORA
INDIA

037

038

EK THONGPRASERT
THAILAND

MANISH ARORA
INDIA

039

040

BOHENTO
SPAIN

MAL-AIMÉE
FRANCE

041

042

ERICA ZAIONTS
UKRAINE

G.V.G.V.
JAPAN

043

044

THE SWEDISH SCHOOL OF TEXTILES
SWEDEN

JUANJO OLIVA
SPAIN

045

046

THE SWEDISH SCHOOL OF TEXTILES
SWEDEN

MALAFACHA BRAND
MEXICO

047

048

THE SWEDISH SCHOOL OF TEXTILES
SWEDEN

ALENA AKHMADULLINA
RUSSIA

049

050

DIANA DORADO
COLOMBIA

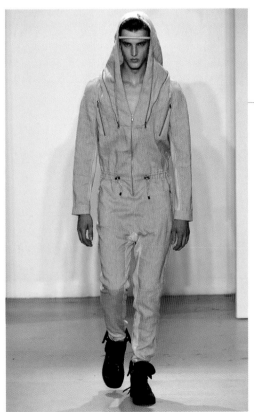

QASIMI
UNITED ARAB EMIRATES

051

052

DIANA DORADO
COLOMBIA

IDA SJÖSTEDT
SWEDEN

053

054

DIANA DORADO
COLOMBIA

CATI SERRÀ
SPAIN

055

056

VICTORIO & LUCCHINO
SPAIN

THE SWEDISH SCHOOL OF TEXTILES
SWEDEN

057

058

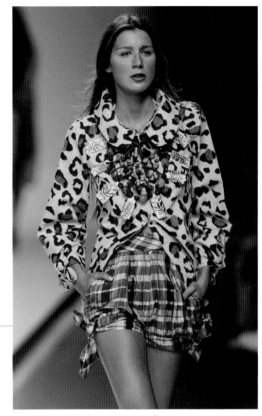

AMERICAN PÉREZ
SPAIN

A.F. VANDEVORST
BELGIUM

059

060

VICTORIO & LUCCHINO
SPAIN

JEAN//PHILLIP
DENMARK

061

062

ALENA AKHMADULLINA
RUSSIA

EWA I WALLA
SWEDEN

063

064

ELENA PRZHONSKAYA
UKRAINE

MAYA HANSEN
SPAIN

065

066

ELENA PRZHONSKAYA
UKRAINE

TSUMORI CHISATO
JAPAN

067

068

VASSILIOS KOSTETSOS
GREECE

CATI SERRÀ
SPAIN

069

070

MAYA HANSEN
SPAIN

ANA LOCKING
SPAIN

071

072

NEREA LURGAIN
SPAIN

MARTIN LAMOTHE
SPAIN

073

074

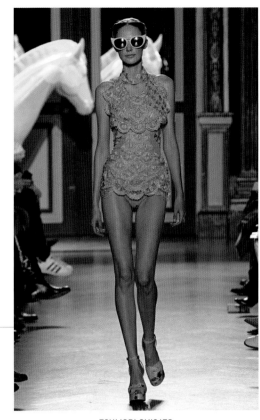

TSUMORI CHISATO
JAPAN

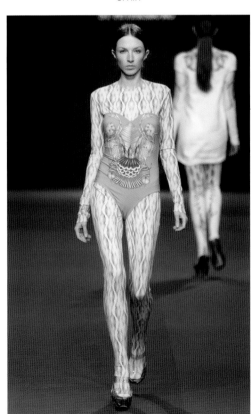

ALENA AKHMADULLINA
RUSSIA

075

076

ALENA AKHMADULLINA
RUSSIA

NEREA LURGAIN
SPAIN

077

078

ALENA AKHMADULLINA
RUSSIA

ION FIZ
SPAIN

079

080

AILANTO
SPAIN

MAL-AIMÉE
FRANCE

081

082

MAL-AIMÉE
FRANCE

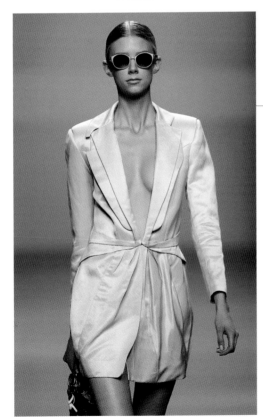

ION FIZ
SPAIN

083

084

QASIMI
UNITED ARAB EMIRATES

ALENA AKHMADULLINA
RUSSIA

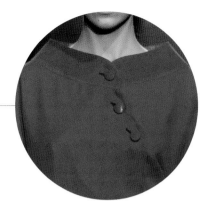

085

086

DESIGNSKOLEN KOLDING
DENMARK

STAS LOPATKIN
RUSSIA

087

088

TSUMORI CHISATO
JAPAN

VICTORIO & LUCCHINO
SPAIN

089

090

EWA I WALLA
SWEDEN

ERICA ZAIONTS
UKRAINE

091

092

QASIMI
UNITED ARAB EMIRATES

NEREA LURGAIN
SPAIN

093

094

DESIGNSKOLEN KOLDING
DENMARK

MANISH ARORA
INDIA

095

096

ERICA ZAIONTS
UKRAINE

TSUMORI CHISATO

JAPAN

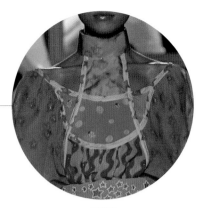

097

098

ALENA AKHMADULLINA

RUSSIA

BIBIAN BLUE

SPAIN

099

100

MALAFACHA BRAND

MEXICO

AGANOVICH
SERBIA/UK

101

102

ANNA MIMINOSHVILI
RUSSIA

LEMONIEZ
SPAIN

103

104

ANTONIO ALVARADO
SPAIN

BOHENTO
SPAIN

105

106

THE SWEDISH SCHOOL OF TEXTILES
SWEDEN

DESIGNSKOLEN KOLDING
DENMARK

107

108

ANTONIO ALVARADO
SPAIN

BOHENTO
SPAIN

109

110

AILANTO
SPAIN

DIMITRI
ITALY

111

112

THE SWEDISH SCHOOL OF TEXTILES
SWEDEN

© Kristian Löveborg

37

ANJARA
SPAIN

113

114

DIMITRI
ITALY

BOHENTO
SPAIN

115

116

A.F. VANDEVORST
BELGIUM

JEAN//PHILLIP
DENMARK

117

118

JULIUS
JAPAN

A.F. VANDEVORST
BELGIUM

119

120

JEAN//PHILLIP
DENMARK

A.F. VANDEVORST
BELGIUM

121

122

ASHER LEVINE
USA

ALENA AKHMADULLINA
RUSSIA

123

124

A.F. VANDEVORST
BELGIUM

SPIJKERS EN SPIJKERS
THE NETHERLANDS

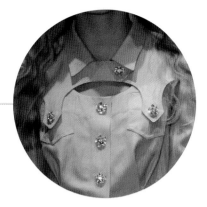

125

126

THE SWEDISH SCHOOL OF TEXTILES
SWEDEN

DESIGNSKOLEN KOLDING
DENMARK

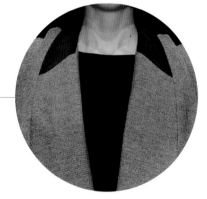

127

128

JEAN//PHILLIP
DENMARK

THE SWEDISH SCHOOL OF TEXTILES
SWEDEN

129

130

BOHENTO
SPAIN

MALAFACHA BRAND
MEXICO

131

132

MANISH ARORA
INDIA

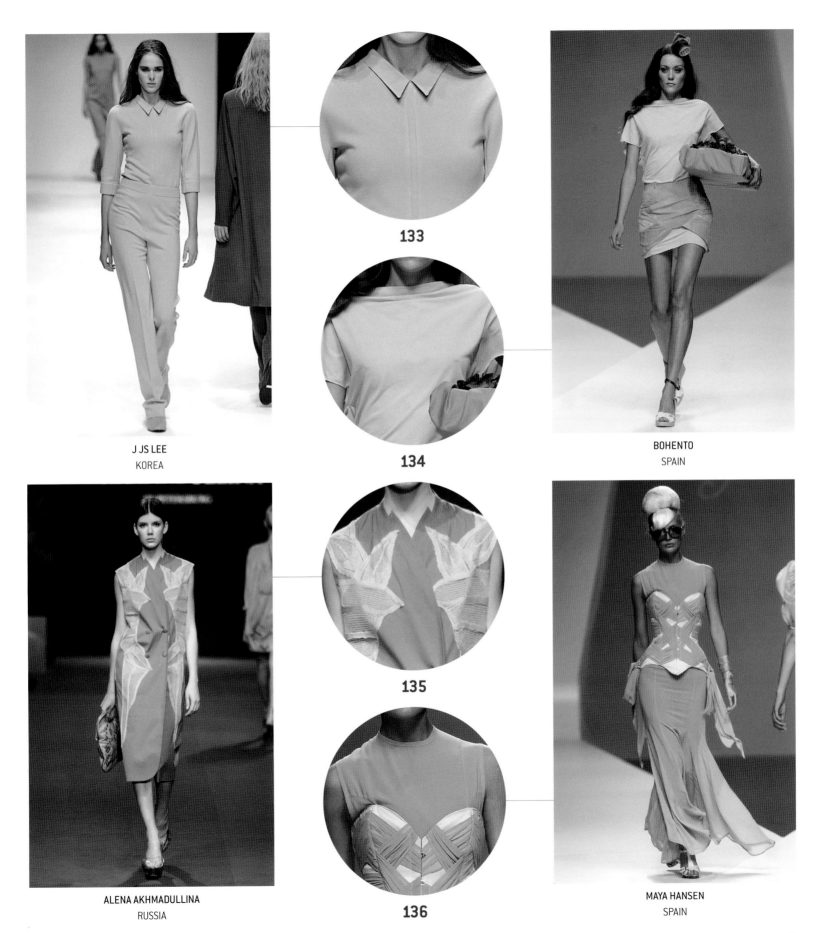

J JS LEE
KOREA

133

134

BOHENTO
SPAIN

ALENA AKHMADULLINA
RUSSIA

135

136

MAYA HANSEN
SPAIN

J JS LEE
KOREA

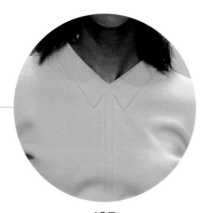

137

138

IDA SJÖSTEDT
SWEDEN

MALAFACHA BRAND
MEXICO

139

140

ERICA ZAIONTS
UKRAINE

MAYA HANSEN
SPAIN

141

142

ANTONIO ALVARADO
SPAIN

MAL-AIMÉE
FRANCE

143

144

MAYA HANSEN
SPAIN

ASHER LEVINE
USA

145

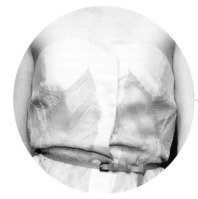

146

ALENA AKHMADULLINA
RUSSIA

ELENA PRZHONSKAYA
UKRAINE

147

148

ASHER LEVINE
USA

CARLOS DÍEZ
SPAIN

149

150

ION FIZ
SPAIN

CAMILLA NORRBACK
FINLAND

© Kristian Löveborg

151

152

SINPATRON
SPAIN

RICARDO DOURADO
PORTUGAL

153

154

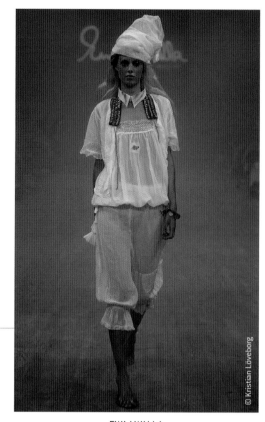

EWA I WALLA
SWEDEN

KARLOTA LASPALAS
SPAIN

155

156

CAMILLA NORRBACK
FINLAND

JULIUS
JAPAN

157

158

GEORGIA HARDINGE
UK

ERICA ZAIONTS
UKRAINE

159

160

HARRIHALIM
INDONESIA

ASGER JUEL LARSEN
DENMARK

161

162

MARK FAST
CANADA

ANJARA
SPAIN

163

164

TSUMORI CHISATO
JAPAN

KRIS VAN ASSCHE
BELGIUM

165

166

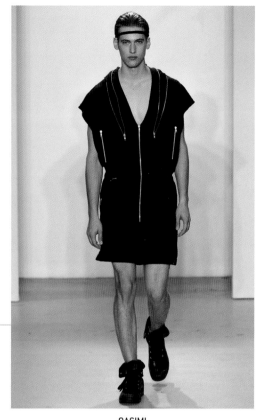

QASIMI
UNITED ARAB EMIRATES

TSUMORI CHISATO
JAPAN

167

168

BORA AKSU
TURKEY

ANNA MIMINOSHVILI
RUSSIA

169

170

SPIJKERS EN SPIJKERS
THE NETHERLANDS

MARK FAST
CANADA

171

172

ERICA ZAIONTS
UKRAINE

HARRIHALIM
INDONESIA

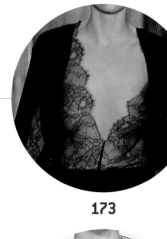

173

174

ANNA MIMINOSHVILI
RUSSIA

HARRIHALIM
INDONESIA

175

176

JULIUS
JAPAN

© Étienne Tordoir

53

J JS LEE
KOREA

177

178

ADA ZANDITON
UK

DESIGNSKOLEN KOLDING
DENMARK

179

180

HARRIHALIM
INDONESIA

QASIMI
UNITED ARAB EMIRATES

181

182

HARRIHALIM
INDONESIA

© Kristian Löveborg

THE SWEDISH SCHOOL OF TEXTILES
SWEDEN

183

184

J JS LEE
KOREA

HARRIHALIM
INDONESIA

185

186

THE SWEDISH SCHOOL OF TEXTILES
SWEDEN

MARK FAST
CANADA

187

188

TSUMORI CHISATO
JAPAN

189

TIM VAN STEENBERGEN

BELGIUM

190

MANISH ARORA

INDIA

191

VLADISLAV AKSENOV

RUSSIA

192

MARK FAST

CANADA

MARK FAST
CANADA

193

194

HARRIHALIM
INDONESIA

CAMILLA NORRBACK
FINLAND

195

196

TSUMORI CHISATO
JAPAN

58

JULIUS
JAPAN

197

198

SPIJKERS EN SPIJKERS
THE NETHERLANDS

DESIGNSKOLEN KOLDING
DENMARK

199

200

JULIUS
JAPAN

201

THE SWEDISH SCHOOL OF TEXTILES
SWEDEN

202

THE SWEDISH SCHOOL OF TEXTILES
SWEDEN

203

MARTA MONTOTO
SPAIN

204

MALINI RAMANI
USA/INDIA

KARLOTA LASPALAS
SPAIN

205

206

BORA AKSU
TURKEY

ELENA SKAKUN
RUSSIA

207

208

VLADISLAV AKSENOV
RUSSIA

ERICA ZAIONTS
UKRAINE

209

210

JEAN//PHILLIP
DENMARK

STAS LOPATKIN
RUSSIA

211

212

JEAN//PHILLIP
DENMARK

ANNA MIMINOSHVILI
RUSSIA

213

214

ELENA SKAKUN
RUSSIA

215

JULIUS
JAPAN

216

ANNA MIMINOSHVILI
RUSSIA

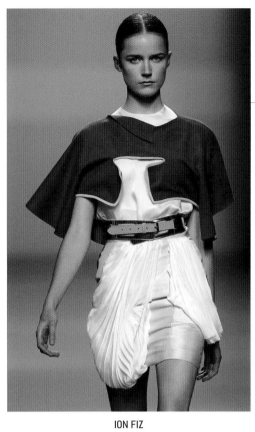

ION FIZ
SPAIN

217

218

TIM VAN STEENBERGEN
BELGIUM

SPIJKERS EN SPIJKERS
THE NETHERLANDS

219

220

LEMONIEZ
SPAIN

AGANOVICH
SERBIA/UK

221

222

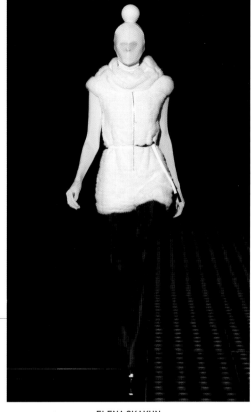

ELENA SKAKUN
RUSSIA

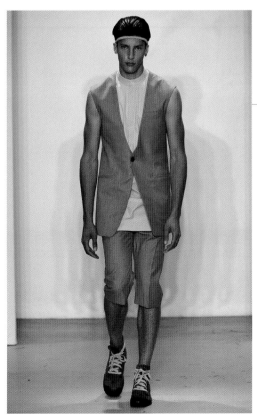

QASIMI
UNITED ARAB EMIRATES

223

224

JULIUS
JAPAN

VASSILIOS KOSTETSOS
GREECE

225

226

QASIMI
UNITED ARAB EMIRATES

JULIUS
JAPAN

227

228

EWA I WALLA
SWEDEN

ION FIZ
SPAIN

229

230

STAS LOPATKIN
RUSSIA

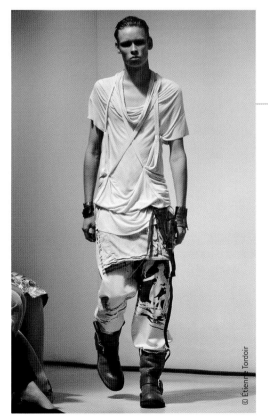

JULIUS
JAPAN

231

232

STAS LOPATKIN
RUSSIA

67

BIBIAN BLUE
SPAIN

233

234

ANNA MIMINOSHVILI
RUSSIA

JULIUS
JAPAN

© Étienne Tordoir

235

236

DIANA DORADO
COLOMBIA

DAWID TOMASZEWSKI
POLAND

237

238

MAL-AIMÉE
FRANCE

ANNA MIMINOSHVILI
RUSSIA

239

240

QASIMI
UNITED ARAB EMIRATES

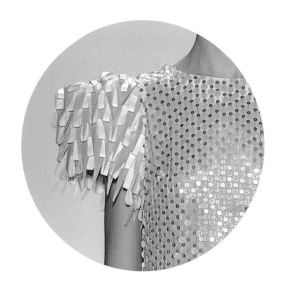

SHOULDERS AND SLEEVES

SCHULTERN UND ÄRMEL

HOMBROS Y MANGAS

Shoulders and sleeves have a prominent role in current trends in fashion. After the subtlety and simplicity of the past two decades, now runways around the world are inundated with the spirit of the eighties with proposals that very much concentrate the entire volume in this area, resulting in daring designs and creative proposals that convey richness and elegance. We include the legendary exaggerated Grace Jones-style shoulder pads, whose revival this century is attributed to the French maison Balmain, and so many others that border on an architectural interpretation, and those that remind us of samurai warrior armor. As for the sleeves, we will see a considerable influence from this period, taking puffed, lantern or gigot sleeves as a reference. Appliqués, epaulets, transparencies, structures, padding and a countless number of techniques are included in the patterns of the most cutting-edge designs discussed in this chapter.

In der aktuellen Mode sind Schultern und Ärmel die großen Protagonisten der Trends. Nach der Subtilität und Einfachheit der vergangenen zwei Jahrzehnte sind die Laufstege heute weltweit von Entwürfen im Sinne der Achtziger überflutet, die sich ganz auf diesen Bereich konzentrieren und zu gewagten Designs und sehr kreativen Modellen führen, die Luxus und Eleganz vermitteln. Wir finden mythische übertriebene Schulterpolster à la Grace Jones, deren Wiederaufkommen in diesem Jahrhundert dem französischen Modehaus Balmain zu verdanken ist, viele andere, die das Architektonische streifen, und jene, die an die Kleidung von Samuraikriegern erinnern. Auch bei den Ärmeln sehen wir einen starken Einfluss jener Zeit in der Anlehnung an Ballon- oder Puffärmel. Applikationen, Epauletten, transparente Elemente, Strukturen, Polster und unzählige weitere Techniken fanden bei den Entwürfen der avantgardistischsten Designs Anwendung, wie wir in diesem Kapitel sehen.

En la moda actual los hombros y las mangas son los grandes protagonistas de las tendencias. Después de la sutileza y simplicidad de las dos últimas décadas, ahora las pasarelas de todo el mundo se inundan del espíritu de los años ochenta con propuestas que concentran todo su volumen en esta zona, dando como resultado arriesgados diseños y propuestas muy creativas que transmiten suntuosidad y elegancia. Encontraremos míticas hombreras exageradas a lo Grace Jones, cuyo relanzamiento en este siglo se le atribuye a la *maison* francesa Balmain, otras tantas que rozan lo arquitectónico y aquellas que rememoran las armaduras de los guerreros samuráis. En cuanto a las mangas, también veremos bastante influencia de esta época, tomando como referencia las mangas abullonadas, las mangas farol o las mangas jamón. Aplicaciones, charreteras, transparencias, estructuras, almohadillados y un incontable número de técnicas tienen cabida en los patrones de los diseños más vanguardistas, como veremos en este capítulo.

ANJARA
SPAIN

241

242

THE SWEDISH SCHOOL OF TEXTILES
SWEDEN

© Kristian Löveborg

BORA AKSU
TURKEY

243

244

MALAFACHA BRAND
MEXICO

© Israel Esparza

MANISH ARORA

INDIA

245

246

TSUMORI CHISATO

JAPAN

MALAFACHA BRAND

MEXICO

247

248

ANA LOCKING

SPAIN

ANA LOCKING
SPAIN

249

250

TSUMORI CHISATO
JAPAN

MALAFACHA BRAND
MEXICO

251

252

MANISH ARORA
INDIA

ANA LOCKING
SPAIN

253

254

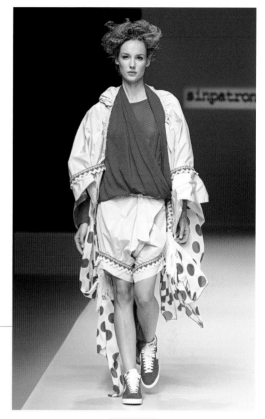

SINPATRON
SPAIN

MALAFACHA BRAND
MEXICO

255

256

A.F. VANDEVORST
BELGIUM

MALAFACHA BRAND
MEXICO

257

258

ANTONIO ALVARADO
SPAIN

THE SWEDISH SCHOOL OF TEXTILES
SWEDEN

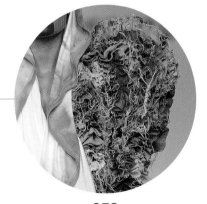

259

260

ION FIZ
SPAIN

ELISA PALOMINO
SPAIN

261

262

AGANOVICH
SERBIA/UK

DIMITRI
ITALY

263

264

VICTORIO & LUCCHINO
SPAIN

265

ANA LOCKING
SPAIN

266

G.V.G.V.
JAPAN

267

VASSILIOS KOSTETSOS
GREECE

268

G.V.G.V.
JAPAN

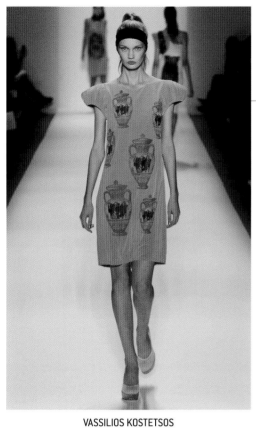

VASSILIOS KOSTETSOS
GREECE

269

270

THE SWEDISH SCHOOL OF TEXTILES
SWEDEN

MALAFACHA BRAND
MEXICO

271

272

DESIGNSKOLEN KOLDING
DENMARK

MANISH ARORA
INDIA

273

274

VASSILIOS KOSTETSOS
GREECE

DESIGNSKOLEN KOLDING
DENMARK

275

276

BEBA'S CLOSET
SPAIN

277

278

VASSILIOS KOSTETSOS
GREECE

DAWID TOMASZEWSKI
POLAND

279

280

ELENA PRZHONSKAYA
UKRAINE

ELENA PRZHONSKAYA
UKRAINE

281

MARTIN LAMOTHE
SPAIN

282

VASSILIOS KOSTETSOS
GREECE

283

ANTONIO ALVARADO
SPAIN

284

ANTONIO ALVARADO
SPAIN

ALENA AKHMADULLINA
RUSSIA

285

286

THE SWEDISH SCHOOL OF TEXTILES
SWEDEN

© Kristian Löveborg

DESIGNSKOLEN KOLDING
DENMARK

287

288

EK THONGPRASERT
THAILAND

ALI CHARISMA
INDONESIA

289

290

VASSILIOS KOSTETSOS
GREECE

MALINI RAMANI
USA/INDIA

291

292

ALI CHARISMA
INDONESIA

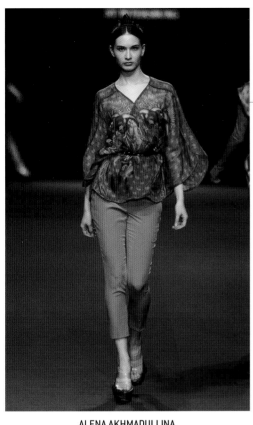

ALENA AKHMADULLINA
RUSSIA

293

294

MALINI RAMANI
USA/INDIA

ELENA PRZHONSKAYA
UKRAINE

295

296

STAS LOPATKIN
RUSSIA

ANNA MIMINOSHVILI
RUSSIA

297

298

ELENA PRZHONSKAYA
UKRAINE

ANNA MIMINOSHVILI
RUSSIA

299

300

MAL-AIMÉE
FRANCE

CATI SERRÀ
SPAIN

301

302

MANISH ARORA
INDIA

ALENA AKHMADULLINA
RUSSIA

303

304

MANISH ARORA
INDIA

ANNA MIMINOSHVILI
RUSSIA

305

306

MANISH ARORA
INDIA

VASSILIOS KOSTETSOS
GREECE

307

308

MAISON MARTIN MARGIELA
FRANCE

MAL-AIMÉE

FRANCE

309

310

MAL-AIMÉE

FRANCE

AMERICAN PÉREZ

SPAIN

311

312

GEORGIA HARDINGE

UK

89

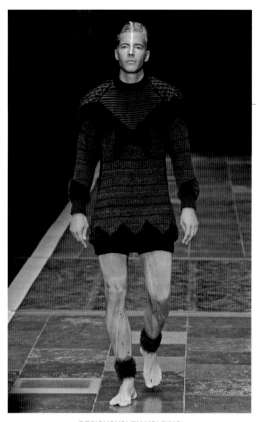

DESIGNSKOLEN KOLDING
DENMARK

313

314

DESIGNSKOLEN KOLDING
DENMARK

© Kristian Löveborg

CAMILLA NORRBACK
FINLAND

315

316

© Israel Esparza

MALAFACHA BRAND
MEXICO

317

318

VASSILIOS KOSTETSOS
GREECE

DESIGNSKOLEN KOLDING
DENMARK

319

320

DESIGNSKOLEN KOLDING
DENMARK

ION FIZ
SPAIN

IDA SJÖSTEDT
SWEDEN

© Kristian Löveborg

321

322

CATI SERRÀ
SPAIN

GEORGIA HARDINGE
UK

323

324

STAS LOPATKIN
RUSSIA

ASHER LEVINE
USA

325

326

DIANA DORADO
COLOMBIA

CATI SERRÀ
SPAIN

327

328

ION FIZ
SPAIN

THE SWEDISH SCHOOL OF TEXTILES
SWEDEN

329

330

© Kristian Löveborg

VASSILIOS KOSTETSOS
GREECE

BEBA'S CLOSET
SPAIN

331

332

DESIGNSKOLEN KOLDING
DENMARK

CAMILLA NORRBACK
FINLAND

333

334

MAL-AIMÉE
FRANCE

BEBA'S CLOSET
SPAIN

335

336

DESIGNSKOLEN KOLDING
DENMARK

95

MANISH ARORA

INDIA

337

338

RICARDO DOURADO

PORTUGAL

VASSILIOS KOSTETSOS

GREECE

339

340

MAYA HANSEN

SPAIN

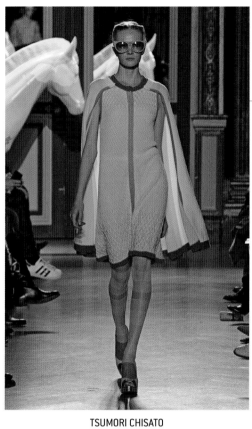

TSUMORI CHISATO

JAPAN

341

342

ALI CHARISMA

INDONESIA

DESIGNSKOLEN KOLDING

DENMARK

343

344

THE SWEDISH SCHOOL OF TEXTILES

SWEDEN

© Kristian Löveborg

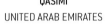

QASIMI
UNITED ARAB EMIRATES

345

346

DESIGNSKOLEN KOLDING
DENMARK

JEAN//PHILLIP
DENMARK

347

348

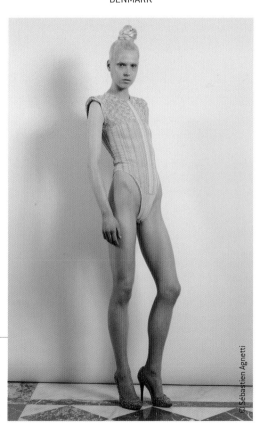

MAL-AIMÉE
FRANCE

© Sébastien Agnetti

349

TSUMORI CHISATO

JAPAN

350

QASIMI

UNITED ARAB EMIRATES

351

SINPATRON

SPAIN

352

VASSILIOS KOSTETSOS

GREECE

IDA SJÖSTEDT
SWEDEN

353

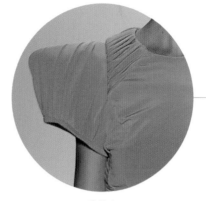

354

VASSILIOS KOSTETSOS
GREECE

JEAN//PHILLIP
DENMARK

355

356

QASIMI
UNITED ARAB EMIRATES

VRL COLLECTION
SPAIN

357

358

VLADISLAV AKSENOV
RUSSIA

VRL COLLECTION
SPAIN

359

360

ASHER LEVINE
USA

DESIGNSKOLEN KOLDING
DENMARK

361

362

ASHER LEVINE
USA

DESIGNSKOLEN KOLDING
DENMARK

363

364

VASSILIOS KOSTETSOS
GREECE

DIMITRI
ITALY

365

366

BERNARD CHANDRAN
MALAYSIA

IDA SJÖSTEDT
SWEDEN

367

368

VASSILIOS KOSTETSOS
GREECE

TIM VAN STEENBERGEN
BELGIUM

369

370

THE SWEDISH SCHOOL OF TEXTILES
SWEDEN

TIM VAN STEENBERGEN
BELGIUM

371

372

SPIJKERS EN SPIJKERS
THE NETHERLANDS

THE SWEDISH SCHOOL OF TEXTILES
SWEDEN

373

374

TSUMORI CHISATO
JAPAN

EWA I WALLA
SWEDEN

375

376

TSUMORI CHISATO
JAPAN

ELISA PALOMINO
SPAIN

377

378

ALI CHARISMA
INDONESIA

TSUMORI CHISATO
JAPAN

379

380

AGANOVICH
SERBIA/UK

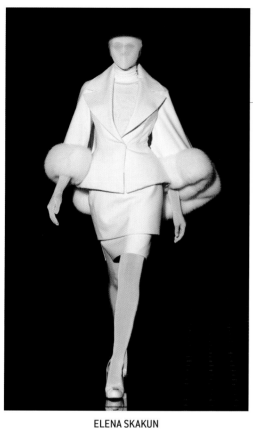

ELENA SKAKUN
RUSSIA

381

382

SPIJKERS EN SPIJKERS
THE NETHERLANDS

VASSILIOS KOSTETSOS
GREECE

383

384

AGANOVICH
SERBIA/UK

BIBIAN BLUE
SPAIN

385

386

STAS LOPATKIN
RUSSIA

MAYA HANSEN
SPAIN

387

388

DAWID TOMASZEWSKI
POLAND

© Mina Gerngross

BIBIAN BLUE
SPAIN

389

390

VASSILIOS KOSTETSOS
GREECE

DESIGNSKOLEN KOLDING
DENMARK

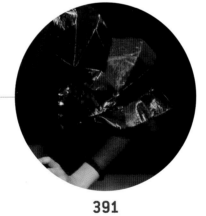

391

ANJARA
SPAIN

392

KRIS VAN ASSCHE
BELGIUM

393

394

MAL-AIMÉE
FRANCE

HARRIHALIM
INDONESIA

395

396

DESIGNSKOLEN KOLDING
DENMARK

110

397

AILANTO
SPAIN

398

MARK FAST
CANADA

399

GEORGIA HARDINGE
UK

400

MARCEL OSTERTAG
GERMANY

QASIMI
UNITED ARAB EMIRATES

401

402

BERNARD CHANDRAN
MALAYSIA

RICARDO DOURADO
PORTUGAL

403

404

CHARLIE LE MINDU
FRANCE

THE SWEDISH SCHOOL OF TEXTILES
SWEDEN

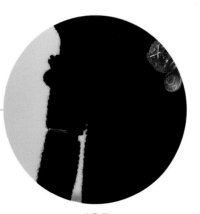

405

406

TSUMORI CHISATO
JAPAN

VLADISLAV AKSENOV
RUSSIA

407

408

ALI CHARISMA
INDONESIA

HARRIHALIM
INDONESIA

409

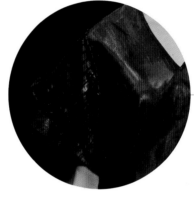

410

DESIGNSKOLEN KOLDING
DENMARK

ANNA MIMINOSHVILI
RUSSIA

411

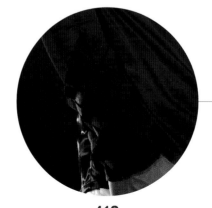

412

VRL COLLECTION
SPAIN

TIM VAN STEENBERGEN
BELGIUM

413

414

DESIGNSKOLEN KOLDING
DENMARK

EWA I WALLA
SWEDEN

415

416

ASGER JUEL LARSEN
DENMARK

WAISTLINES

TAILLEN

CINTURAS

The waistline is paramount when designing garments. Determining the shape and design will completely change the silhouette of a look. The use of waistbands causes an illusory effect in many cases: when it is not in line with the actual position of the waist, and it lies either above or below it, this can visually lengthen the legs, enhance the bust or highlight the hips. This chapter shows the different details and shapes used by designers in this area to enhance both the female and male figure, with references to the forties with their very high waistlines that stylize the figure, other models represent the fifties, where the waist is defined in a more marked manner, balancing out the figure evenly between the hip and bust, Marilyn-style. Low waistlines, gathers, appliqués, seams, sashes, corsets and belts complement and highlight waistbands that are featured in this book.

Die Taille ist ein wesentlicher Teil, der beim Entwurf von Kleidern zu beachten ist. Die Festlegung von Form und Design kann die Silhouette eines Looks vollkommen verändern. Die Taille verursacht in vielen Fällen eine illusorische Wirkung: wenn vermieden wird, dass sie mit der wirklichen Position der Taille übereinstimmt und sie sich darüber oder darunter befindet, wird eine optische Verlängerung der Beine erreicht, werden die Brust oder die Hüften besonders betont. In diesem Kapitel werden die unterschiedlichen Details und Formen gezeigt, die in diesem Bereich von Designern angewandt werden, um sowohl die weibliche als auch die männliche Figur zu betonen. Wir zeigen Referenzen an den puristischen Stil der Vierziger mit sehr hoher Taille, der die Figur stilisiert. Andere Modelle entführen uns in die Fünfziger, als die Taille auf extremere Art hervorgehoben und die Silhouette à la Marilyn in der Mitte geteilt wurde. Niedrige Taillen, Knitter, Applikationen, Nähte, Schärpen, Korsetts und Gürtel ergänzen und betonen die Taillen, die im Folgenden gezeigt werden.

La cintura es una parte fundamental a tener en cuenta en el diseño de las prendas. Determinar su forma y su diseño cambiará por completo la silueta de un *look*. El uso de las cinturillas causa un efecto ilusorio en muchos casos: cuando se evita que coincida con la posición real de la cintura, quedando por encima o por debajo de esta, se consigue prolongar visualmente las piernas, potenciar el busto o resaltar la cadera. En este capítulo se muestran los diferentes detalles y formas aplicados por los diseñadores en esta zona para realzar tanto la figura femenina como la masculina. Mostramos referencias al más puro estilo años cuarenta con cinturas muy altas que estilizan la figura. Otros modelos nos llevan a los años cincuenta, donde la cintura se marca de una manera más extremada, repartiendo el volumen de modo equilibrado entre la cadera y el busto, a lo Marilyn. Cinturas bajas, fruncidos, aplicaciones, costuras, fajines, corsés y cinturones complementan y hacen más vistosas las cinturillas que se muestran a continuación.

ANJARA
SPAIN

417

418

JULIUS
JAPAN

MALAFACHA BRAND
MEXICO

419

420

MARCEL OSTERTAG
GERMANY

G.V.G.V.
JAPAN

421

422

HASAN HEJAZI
UK

CATI SERRÀ
SPAIN

423

424

THE SWEDISH SCHOOL OF TEXTILES
SWEDEN

© Kristian Löveborg

119

G.V.G.V.
JAPAN

425

426

MARCEL OSTERTAG
GERMANY

© Kristian Löveborg

THE SWEDISH SCHOOL OF TEXTILES
SWEDEN

427

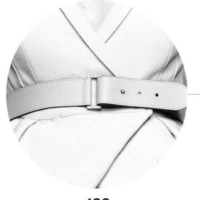

428

ANA LOCKING
SPAIN

DESIGNSKOLEN KOLDING
DENMARK

429

430

G.V.G.V.
JAPAN

DESIGNSKOLEN KOLDING
DENMARK

431

432

ANA LOCKING
SPAIN

MALAFACHA BRAND
MEXICO

433

434

ANA LOCKING
SPAIN

DIMITRI
ITALY

435

436

MALAFACHA BRAND
MEXICO

G.V.G.V.
JAPAN

437

438

CATI SERRÀ
SPAIN

ALENA AKHMADULLINA
RUSSIA

439

440

BOHENTO
SPAIN

ANJARA
SPAIN

441

442

EWA I WALLA
SWEDEN

ERICA ZAIONTS
UKRAINE

443

444

MALAFACHA BRAND
MEXICO

MAISON MARTIN MARGIELA
FRANCE

445

446

ALI CHARISMA
INDONESIA

ERICA ZAIONTS
UKRAINE

447

448

ANNA MIMINOSHVILI
RUSSIA

MAL-AIMÉE
FRANCE

449

450

ANNA MIMINOSHVILI
RUSSIA

MANISH ARORA
INDIA

451

452

RICARDO DOURADO
PORTUGAL

BEBA'S CLOSET
SPAIN

453

454

CATI SERRÀ
SPAIN

CATI SERRÀ
SPAIN

455

456

ELENA PRZHONSKAYA
UKRAINE

BEBA'S CLOSET
SPAIN

457

458

ELENA PRZHONSKAYA
UKRAINE

459

460

DESIGNSKOLEN KOLDING
DENMARK

EK THONGPRASERT
THAILAND

DESIGNSKOLEN KOLDING
DENMARK

461

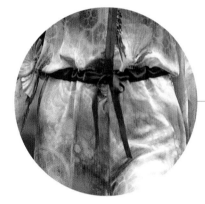

462

IDA SJÖSTEDT
SWEDEN

© Kristian Löveborg

ASHER LEVINE
USA

463

464

AILANTO
SPAIN

JEAN//PHILLIP
DENMARK

465

466

BOHENTO
SPAIN

RICARDO DOURADO
PORTUGAL

467

468

CARLOS DÍEZ
SPAIN

EWA I WALLA
SWEDEN

469

470

CATI SERRÀ
SPAIN

JEAN//PHILLIP
DENMARK

471

472

RICARDO DOURADO
PORTUGAL

131

AILANTO
SPAIN

473

474

EWA I WALLA
SWEDEN

CAMILLA NORRBACK
FINLAND

475

476

AILANTO
SPAIN

KRIS VAN ASSCHE
BELGIUM

477

478

DESIGNSKOLEN KOLDING
DENMARK

EK THONGPRASERT
THAILAND

479

480

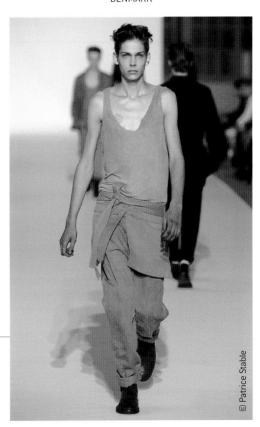

KRIS VAN ASSCHE
BELGIUM

© Patrice Stable

133

NEREA LURGAIN
SPAIN

481

482

QASIMI
UNITED ARAB EMIRATES

ASHER LEVINE
USA

483

484

AILANTO
SPAIN

ANNA MIMINOSHVILI
RUSSIA

485

486

TIM VAN STEENBERGEN
BELGIUM

VLADISLAV AKSENOV
RUSSIA

487

488

TSUMORI CHISATO
JAPAN

KRIS VAN ASSCHE
BELGIUM

489

490

DESIGNSKOLEN KOLDING
DENMARK

ELENA SKAKUN
RUSSIA

491

492

ERICA ZAIONTS
UKRAINE

JEAN//PHILLIP
DENMARK

493

494

STAS LOPATKIN
RUSSIA

KRIS VAN ASSCHE
BELGIUM

495

496

HARRIHALIM
INDONESIA

JEAN//PHILLIP
DENMARK

497

498

ANNA MIMINOSHVILI
RUSSIA

JULIUS
JAPAN

499

500

TIM VAN STEENBERGEN
BELGIUM

© Étienne Tordoir

© Étienne Tordoir

ERICA ZAIONTS
UKRAINE

501

502

THE SWEDISH SCHOOL OF TEXTILES
SWEDEN

SPIJKERS EN SPIJKERS
THE NETHERLANDS

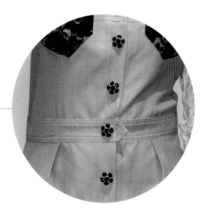

503

504

AILANTO
SPAIN

POCKETS, ZIPPERS AND BUTTONS

TASCHEN, REISSVERSCHLÜSSE UND KNÖPFE

BOLSILLOS, CIERRES Y BOTONES

This section compiles together different details, which primarily had a practical use and that currently, in many cases, have a decorative role: pockets, buttons, snap rings, bundles, zippers, hooks, clips, Velcro and buckles. Many of these started off as working or military accessories, however because of their functionality they were incorporated into civilian clothes and consequently into current fashion trends. Perhaps the zipper is the accessory that has evolved the most, invented by Gideon Sundback in 1913 and patented in 1917 as hookless fastener, in 1923 the Goodrich Corporation coined the onomatopoeic name zipper. Today there are a wide variety of zippers on the market, such as waterproof or invisible zippers, and available in materials such as polyester or metal alloys. We will see how the influence of zippers on eighties-style leather jackets is very much present in fashion today, giving many looks a more punk and rock style.

In diesem Abschnitt haben wir verschiedene Details zusammengefasst; Elemente, die ursprünglich einen rein praktischen Nutzen hatten und inzwischen in vielen Fällen auch eine dekorative Funktion erfüllen: Taschen, Knöpfe, Haken, Schnallen, Reißverschlüsse, Schnüre, Klettverschlüsse und Gürtelschnallen. Viele dieser Elemente entstanden in der Arbeitswelt oder im Militär und wurden aufgrund ihrer Funktionalität in die zivile Kleidung übernommen, also auch in die Mode. Eines, das sich am stärksten entwickelt hat, mag der Reißverschluss sein, der 1913 von Gideon Sundback erfunden und 1917 als „Hookless Fastener" (hakenloser Verschluss) patentiert wurde; die Goodrich Corporation prägte 1923 den lautmalerischen Namen „Zipper". Heute gibt es eine große Vielfalt an Reißverschlüssen, darunter wasserdichte oder unsichtbare, aus Polyester oder Metalllegierungen. Wir sehen, wie präsent der Einfluss der Reißverschlüsse von den Lederjacken der Achtziger in der aktuellen Mode ist und vielen Looks einen punkigen oder rockigen Hauch verleiht, mit dem diese Details verbunden sind.

En este apartado hemos reunido diferentes detalles; elementos que en sus inicios tuvieron un uso totalmente práctico y que, actualmente, en muchos casos, tienen además una función decorativa: bolsillos, botones, mosquetones, atados, cremalleras, corchetes, presillas, velcros y hebillas. Muchos de estos elementos nacieron en el ámbito laboral o militar y, por su funcionalidad, se fueron incorporando a la ropa civil y por lo tanto a la moda. Tal vez uno de los que más haya evolucionado sea la cremallera, inventada por Gideon Sundback en 1913 y patentada en 1917 como *hookless fastener* ('broche sin gancho'); la Goodrich Corporation acuñó en 1923 el nombre onomatopéyico *zipper*. Hoy encontramos una gran variedad de cremalleras en el mercado, como las impermeables o las invisibles, y en materiales como el poliéster o las aleaciones de metal. Veremos como la influencia de las cremalleras en las chupas de cuero ochenteras está muy presente en la moda actual, aportándole a muchos *looks* el aire punk y rock con el que se vinculan estos detalles.

ANJARA
SPAIN

505

506

ANTONIO ALVARADO
SPAIN

MARCEL OSTERTAG
GERMANY

507

508

MALAFACHA BRAND
MEXICO

509

LEMONIEZ
SPAIN

510

MALAFACHA BRAND
MEXICO

511

SPIJKERS EN SPIJKERS
THE NETHERLANDS

512

MALAFACHA BRAND
MEXICO

© Israel Esparza

MANISH ARORA
INDIA

513

514

MALAFACHA BRAND
MEXICO

AILANTO
SPAIN

515

516

MALAFACHA BRAND
MEXICO

144

ANA LOCKING
SPAIN

517

518

ALENA AKHMADULLINA
RUSSIA

MARTIN LAMOTHE
SPAIN

519

520

ANA LOCKING
SPAIN

ANTONIO ALVARADO
SPAIN

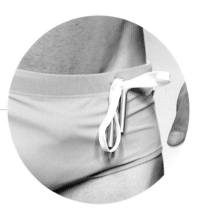

521

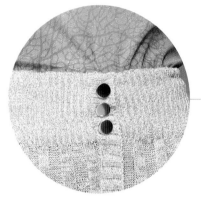

522

CATI SERRÀ
SPAIN

QASIMI
UNITED ARAB EMIRATES

523

524

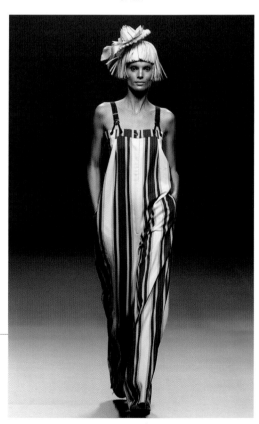

CARLOS DÍEZ
SPAIN

DESIGNSKOLEN KOLDING
DENMARK

525

526

ALENA AKHMADULLINA
RUSSIA

MARTIN LAMOTHE
SPAIN

527

528

DESIGNSKOLEN KOLDING
DENMARK

EWA I WALLA
SWEDEN

529

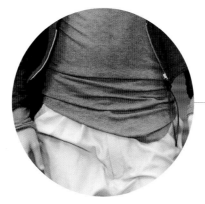

530

JEAN//PHILLIP
DENMARK

KARLOTA LASPALAS
SPAIN

531

532

ANTONIO ALVARADO
SPAIN

KARLOTA LASPALAS
SPAIN

533

534

THE SWEDISH SCHOOL OF TEXTILES
SWEDEN

ELENA PRZHONSKAYA
UKRAINE

535

536

MAISON MARTIN MARGIELA
FRANCE

JEAN//PHILLIP
DENMARK

537

538

ELENA PRZHONSKAYA
UKRAINE

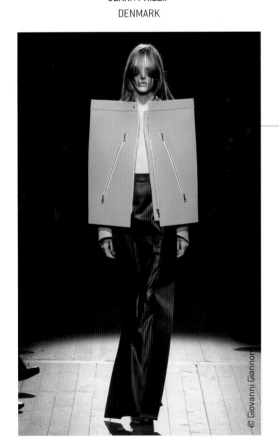

MAISON MARTIN MARGIELA
FRANCE

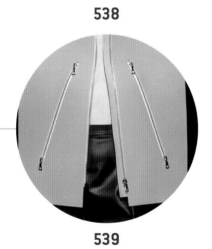

539

540

JEAN//PHILLIP
DENMARK

HASAN HEJAZI
UK

541

542

543

544

RICARDO DOURADO
PORTUGAL

RICARDO DOURADO
PORTUGAL

DESIGNSKOLEN KOLDING
DENMARK

ANA LOCKING
SPAIN

545

546

RICARDO DOURADO
PORTUGAL

ALENA AKHMADULLINA
RUSSIA

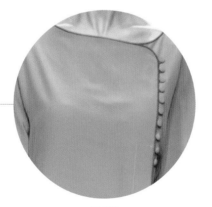

547

548

EK THONGPRASERT
THAILAND

DESIGNSKOLEN KOLDING
DENMARK

549

550

SINPATRON
SPAIN

EK THONGPRASERT
THAILAND

551

552

ANA LOCKING
SPAIN

AILANTO
SPAIN

553

554

ELENA PRZHONSKAYA
UKRAINE

LEMONIEZ
SPAIN

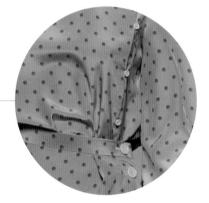

555

556

MALAFACHA BRAND
MEXICO

ANTONIO ALVARADO
SPAIN

557

558

ELENA PRZHONSKAYA
UKRAINE

HASAN HEJAZI
UK

559

560

DESIGNSKOLEN KOLDING
DENMARK

LEMONIEZ
SPAIN

561

562

RICARDO DOURADO
PORTUGAL

EWA I WALLA
SWEDEN

© Kristian Löveborg

563

564

KARLOTA LASPALAS
SPAIN

RICARDO DOURADO
PORTUGAL

565

566

BIBIAN BLUE
SPAIN

567

LEMONIEZ
SPAIN

568

RICARDO DOURADO
PORTUGAL

ANTONIO ALVARADO
SPAIN

569

570

MAL-AIMÉE
FRANCE

NEREA LURGAIN
SPAIN

571

572

JUANJO OLIVA
SPAIN

EK THONGPRASERT

THAILAND

573

574

JULIUS

JAPAN

© Étienne Tordoir

ALENA AKHMADULLINA

RUSSIA

575

576

QASIMI

UNITED ARAB EMIRATES

159

KRIS VAN ASSCHE
BELGIUM

577

578

ION FIZ
SPAIN

EWA I WALLA
SWEDEN

579

580

QASIMI
UNITED ARAB EMIRATES

RICARDO DOURADO
PORTUGAL

581

582

EWA I WALLA
SWEDEN

OMAR KASHOURA
UK

583

584

DESIGNSKOLEN KOLDING
DENMARK

© Mina Gerngross

DAWID TOMASZEWSKI
POLAND

585

586

ASHER LEVINE
USA

ELENA SKAKUN
RUSSIA

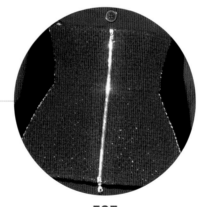

587

588

ASHER LEVINE
USA

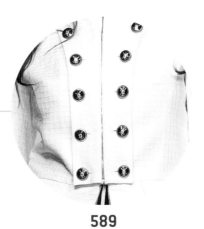

589

STAS LOPATKIN

RUSSIA

590

QASIMI

UNITED ARAB EMIRATES

591

TSUMORI CHISATO

JAPAN

592

SINPATRON

SPAIN

ASHER LEVINE
USA

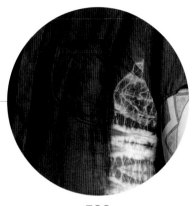

593

594

DESIGNSKOLEN KOLDING
DENMARK

ASHER LEVINE
USA

595

596

JEAN//PHILLIP
DENMARK

ASHER LEVINE
USA

597

598

JULIUS
JAPAN

© Étienne Tordoir

JEAN//PHILLIP
DENMARK

599

600

JULIUS
JAPAN

© Étienne Tordoir

601

KRIS VAN ASSCHE
BELGIUM

602

EWA I WALLA
SWEDEN

603

QASIMI
UNITED ARAB EMIRATES

604

VLADISLAV AKSENOV
RUSSIA

DESIGNSKOLEN KOLDING
DENMARK

605

606

JEAN//PHILLIP
DENMARK

VLADISLAV AKSENOV
RUSSIA

607

608

SPIJKERS EN SPIJKERS
THE NETHERLANDS

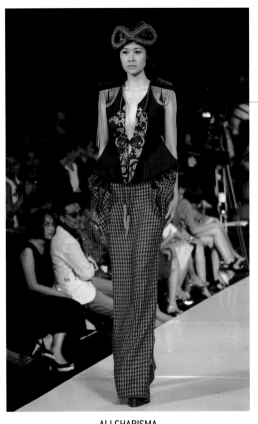

ALI CHARISMA
INDONESIA

609

610

ASGER JUEL LARSEN
DENMARK

DESIGNSKOLEN KOLDING
DENMARK

611

612

VLADISLAV AKSENOV
RUSSIA

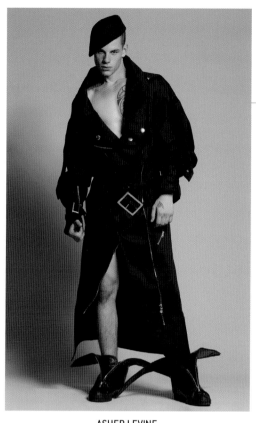

ASHER LEVINE
USA

613

614

KRIS VAN ASSCHE
BELGIUM

CAMILLA NORRBACK
FINLAND

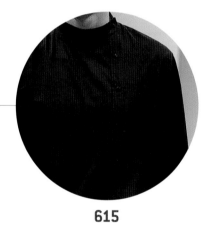

615

616

KARLOTA LASPALAS
SPAIN

169

GATHERING AND DRAPING

FALTEN, KNITTER UND RAFFUNGEN

FRUNCIDOS Y DRAPEADOS

Gathering and draping are techniques that give garments an elegant and romantic look, owing to how the fabric hangs and the decorative effects that gathers create.

Although both are old sewing techniques that date back years and draping, for example, was always considered as a technique linked to haute couture, in current fashion trends both techniques have experienced a resurgence, as discussed throughout this chapter. Gathering, a French technique that involves creating fine creases in the fabric, is very much present in sleeves, waistlines and necklines, creating floral motifs or other embellishments. Draping, which traditionally uses fabrics such as satin, crepe, chiffon or georgette, now can be achieved with more sporty fabrics like cotton and elastane. With some other fabrics, the beauty of the drape and the effect of the how the fabric hangs will occur either by purposely adding more material or by stretching on the bias. In this chapter we will study a selection of the simplest gathers and drapes to more elaborate examples of these old sewing techniques.

Falten, Knitter und Raffungen sind Techniken, die Kleidern ein elegantes und romantisches Aussehen verleihen, bedingt durch das Fallen des Stoffes bei Drapierungen und die so dekorative Wirkung von Falten. Obwohl beide Nähtechniken sehr alt sind und zum Beispiel Raffungen immer als hohe Nähkunsttechnik galten, erleben sie in den Trends der aktuellen Mode eine Wiederbelebung, wie wir in diesem Kapitel sehen. Das Plissieren, eine französische Technik, bei der der Stoff so zurückgelegt wird, dass kleine Falten entstehen, ist an Ärmeln, Taillen und Krägen wieder sehr verbreitet, wodurch florale Muster oder andere Ornamente geschaffen werden. Drapierungen, für die klassischerweise Stoffe wie Satin, Krepp, Chiffon oder Georgette verwendet wurden, haben sich weiterentwickelt und werden heute auch bei sportlicheren Materialien wie Baumwolle oder Elastan angewandt. Doch ganz gleich bei welchem Gewebe, die Anmut von Drapierungen und die Wirkung des fallenden Stoffes entfalten sich gut, wenn mehr Stoff verwendet wird und er schön über die Schrägstreifen fällt. In diesem Kapitel sehen wir alles – von sehr einfachen Falten und Raffungen bis hin zu den ausgefeiltesten Proben dieser alten Nähtechniken.

El fruncido y el drapeado son técnicas que aportan a las prendas un aspecto elegante y romántico, debido a la caída de la tela que proporcionan los drapeados y los efectos tan decorativos que provocan los fruncidos. Aunque ambas técnicas de costura son muy antiguas y el drapeado, por ejemplo, siempre se consideró una técnica ligada a la alta costura, ambas han experimentado un resurgimiento en las tendencias de la moda actual, como veremos a lo largo de este capítulo. El fruncido, una técnica francesa que consiste en recoger la tela para crear en ella pequeñas arrugas, lo veremos muy presente en mangas, cinturas y cuellos, creando motivos florales u otros ornamentos. Los drapeados, para los que clásicamente se han utilizado telas como el raso, el crespón, el chifón o el georgette, se desarrollan ahora con telas más *sport*, como el algodón o el elastán. Con unos u otros tejidos, la gracia del drapeado, el efecto de caída, se producirá o dando más tela a propósito, o estirándola por el bies. En este capítulo veremos desde los fruncidos y drapeados más sencillos hasta elaboradísimas muestras de estas antiguas técnicas de costura.

ANJARA
SPAIN

617

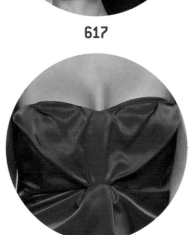

618

BEBA'S CLOSET
SPAIN

© Kristian Löveborg

THE SWEDISH SCHOOL OF TEXTILES
SWEDEN

619

620

CARLOS DÍEZ
SPAIN

LEMONIEZ
SPAIN

621

622

THE SWEDISH SCHOOL OF TEXTILES
SWEDEN

BEBA'S CLOSET
SPAIN

623

624

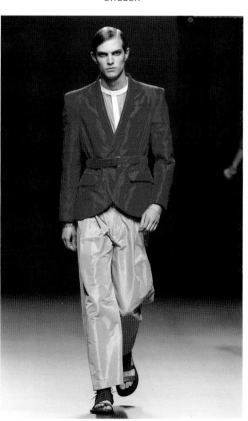

ANA LOCKING
SPAIN

VICTORIO & LUCCHINO
SPAIN

625

626

JUANJO OLIVA
SPAIN

CARLOS DÍEZ
SPAIN

627

628

VICTORIO & LUCCHINO
SPAIN

THE SWEDISH SCHOOL OF TEXTILES
SWEDEN

629

630

VICTORIO & LUCCHINO
SPAIN

VICTORIO & LUCCHINO
SPAIN

631

632

THE SWEDISH SCHOOL OF TEXTILES
SWEDEN

© Kristian Löveborg

175

THE SWEDISH SCHOOL OF TEXTILES
SWEDEN

633

634

VICTORIO & LUCCHINO
SPAIN

MARTIN LAMOTHE
SPAIN

635

636

ELISA PALOMINO
SPAIN

176

VICTORIO & LUCCHINO
SPAIN

637

638

AGANOVICH
SERBIA/UK

© Mina Gerngross

DAWID TOMASZEWSKI
POLAND

639

640

BEBA'S CLOSET
SPAIN

VICTORIO & LUCCHINO
SPAIN

641

642

TSUMORI CHISATO
JAPAN

ANA LOCKING
SPAIN

543

644

DIANA DORADO
COLOMBIA

NEREA LURGAIN
SPAIN

645

646

GEORGIA HARDINGE
UK

ION FIZ
SPAIN

647

648

VASSILIOS KOSTETSOS
GREECE

VICTORIO & LUCCHINO
SPAIN

649

650

TIM VAN STEENBERGEN
BELGIUM

VICTORIO & LUCCHINO
SPAIN

651

652

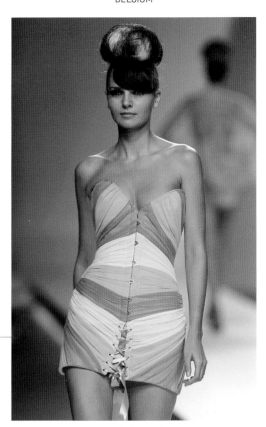

MAYA HANSEN
SPAIN

EWA I WALLA
SWEDEN

653

654

MALAFACHA BRAND
MEXICO

EWA I WALLA
SWEDEN

655

656

ANJARA
SPAIN

© Kristian Löveborg

BOHENTO
SPAIN

657

658

A.F. VANDEVORST
BELGIUM

AILANTO
SPAIN

659

660

AMERICAN PÉREZ
SPAIN

JUANJO OLIVA
SPAIN

661

662

MARTIN LAMOTHE
SPAIN

GEORGIA HARDINGE
UK

663

664

TSUMORI CHISATO
JAPAN

MAYA HANSEN
SPAIN

665

666

JUANJO OLIVA
SPAIN

MALAFACHA BRAND
MEXICO

667

668

EWA I WALLA
SWEDEN

© Kristian Löveborg

ELENA PRZHONSKAYA
UKRAINE

669

670

BEBA'S CLOSET
SPAIN

KARLOTA LASPALAS
SPAIN

671

672

RICARDO DOURADO
PORTUGAL

HARRIHALIM
INDONESIA

673

674

RICARDO DOURADO
PORTUGAL

DESIGNSKOLEN KOLDING
DENMARK

675

676

RICARDO DOURADO
PORTUGAL

DIANA DORADO
COLOMBIA

677

678

TIM VAN STEENBERGEN
BELGIUM

JUANJO OLIVA
SPAIN

679

680

GEORGIA HARDINGE
UK

ELENA SKAKUN
RUSSIA

681

682

SINPATRON
SPAIN

BOHENTO
SPAIN

683

684

DAWID TOMASZEWSKI
POLAND

© Mina Gerngross

A.F. VANDEVORST
BELGIUM

685

686

JEAN//PHILLIP
DENMARK

THE SWEDISH SCHOOL OF TEXTILES
SWEDEN

687

688

A.F. VANDEVORST
BELGIUM

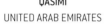

QASIMI

UNITED ARAB EMIRATES

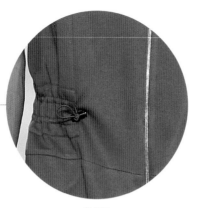

689

690

JUANJO OLIVA

SPAIN

JULIUS

JAPAN

691

692

NEREA LURGAIN

SPAIN

EWA I WALLA
SWEDEN

693

694

ION FIZ
SPAIN

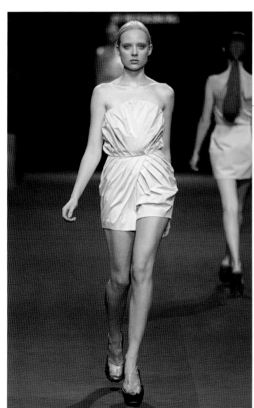

ALENA AKHMADULLINA
RUSSIA

695

696

JEAN//PHILLIP
DENMARK

ERICA ZAIONTS
UKRAINE

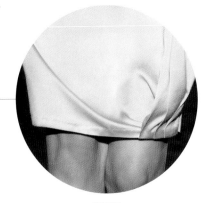

697

698

THE SWEDISH SCHOOL OF TEXTILES
SWEDEN

© Kristian Löveborg

ASHER LEVINE
USA

699

700

THE SWEDISH SCHOOL OF TEXTILES
SWEDEN

© Kristian Löveborg

ANJARA
SPAIN

701

702

TIM VAN STEENBERGEN
BELGIUM

ALENA AKHMADULLINA
RUSSIA

703

704

JEAN//PHILLIP
DENMARK

© Étienne Tordoir

GEORGIA HARDINGE
UK

705

706

DESIGNSKOLEN KOLDING
DENMARK

ANJARA
SPAIN

707

708

A.F. VANDEVORST
BELGIUM

ALI CHARISMA
INDONESIA

709

710

BIBIAN BLUE
SPAIN

A.F. VANDEVORST
BELGIUM

711

712

EWA I WALLA
SWEDEN

195

ASHER LEVINE
USA

ANJARA
SPAIN

713

714

715

716

TIM VAN STEENBERGEN
BELGIUM

TIM VAN STEENBERGEN
BELGIUM

VASSILIOS KOSTETSOS
GREECE

717

718

TIM VAN STEENBERGEN
BELGIUM

ERICA ZAIONTS
UKRAINE

719

720

ELENA PRZHONSKAYA
UKRAINE

197

PLEATS AND FLOUNCES

PLISSEES, RÜSCHEN UND BESÄTZE

PLISADOS Y VOLANTES

This chapter discusses the details of the proposals that stand out for their use of timeless and feminine flounces or the elegance offered by pleats. Flounces, present on runways around the world year after year, especially in spring and summer, are displayed in dozens of different ways. We will study a selection from small flounces, which add a finishing touch to simple garments, to overelaborate voluminous flounces contributing to a sumptuous, vibrant look. They are perfect to provide volume or flight to skirts, dresses, sleeves and collars in delicate fabrics such as chiffon, organza, silk and tulle. Couture designers and experts such as Valentino and Galliano have traditionally drawn inspiration from the influence of Flamenco fashion, which is famous for its feminine flounces. On these pages you will be able to see some of the latest work from the Spanish designers Victorio & Lucchino, the innovative heirs to this art. In addition to the combination of these elements, we will take a look at other techniques such as pintucks and frills.

In diesem Kapitel analysieren wir die Details der Entwürfe, die durch die Verwendung der zeitlosen und femininen Volants oder den eleganten Touch von Plissees hervorstechen. Die Volants, die Jahr für Jahr auf den Laufstegen der ganzen Welt vertreten sind, insbesondere in der Frühjahr-Sommer-Saison, zeigen sich in unzähligen unterschiedlichen Formen. Wir sehen hier kleine Volants, die als zierender Abschluss einfacher Kleider dienen, bis hin zu verspielten vielschichtigen Modellen, die dem Look ein luxuriöses und schwingendes Aussehen verleihen. Ihre Verwendung als Mittel, um Röcken, Kleidern, Ärmeln und Krägen mehr Volumen und ein Schweben zu verleihen, gelingt perfekt mit besonders feinen Stoffen, wie Gaze, Organza, Seide und Tüll. Der Einfluss der Flamenco-Mode, die durch das Feminine ihrer Volants gekennzeichnet ist, diente großen Designern und Modeschöpfern wie Valentino oder Galliano von jeher als Inspiration. Auf den folgenden Seiten sehen wir einige der neuesten Kreationen der Spanier Victorio & Lucchino, den innovativen Erben dieser Kunst. Neben der Kombination dieser Elemente stellen wir auch andere, wie Biesen, Säume oder Krausen heraus.

En este capítulo analizaremos los detalles de las propuestas que destacan por el uso de los eternos y femeninos volantes o por el toque elegante que proporcionan los plisados. Los volantes, presentes en las pasarelas de todo el mundo año tras año, sobre todo en las temporadas de primavera-verano, se muestran en decenas de formas distintas. Veremos desde pequeños volantes, que sirven como remate a prendas sencillas, a superposiciones recargadas que aportan al *look* un aspecto suntuoso y vibrante. Su uso como herramienta para aportar volumen o vuelo a faldas, vestidos, mangas y cuellos es perfecto en tejidos que destacan por su delicadeza, como gasas, organzas, sedas y tules. La influencia de la moda flamenca, que se caracteriza por la feminidad de sus volantes, ha servido tradicionalmente de inspiración para grandes diseñadores y maestros de la costura como Valentino o Galliano. En estas páginas veremos algunos de los últimos diseños de los españoles Victorio & Lucchino, los innovadores herederos de este arte. Además de la combinación de estos elementos, destacaremos otros, como lorzas, jaretas o chorreras.

DIMITRI
ITALY

721

722

MANISH ARORA
INDIA

MALAFACHA BRAND
MEXICO

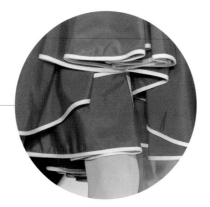

723

724

AMERICAN PÉREZ
SPAIN

MANISH ARORA
INDIA

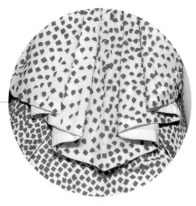

725

726

ANA LOCKING
SPAIN

AMERICAN PÉREZ
SPAIN

727

728

JUANJO OLIVA
SPAIN

VICTORIO & LUCCHINO
SPAIN

729

730

MALAFACHA BRAND
MEXICO

MALAFACHA BRAND
MEXICO

731

732

BEBA'S CLOSET
SPAIN

© Israel Esparza

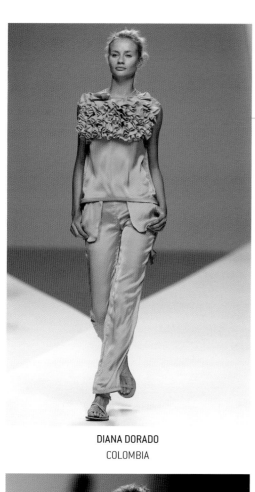

DIANA DORADO
COLOMBIA

733

734

MANISH ARORA
INDIA

DIANA DORADO
COLOMBIA

735

736

IDA SJÖSTEDT
SWEDEN

DIANA DORADO
COLOMBIA

737

738

ION FIZ
SPAIN

AILANTO
SPAIN

739

740

ELISA PALOMINO
SPAIN

ION FIZ
SPAIN

741

742

ELISA PALOMINO
SPAIN

743

DIANA DORADO
COLOMBIA

744

BEBA'S CLOSET
SPAIN

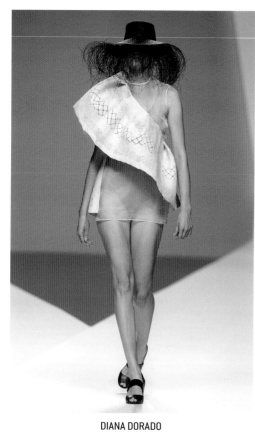

DIANA DORADO
COLOMBIA

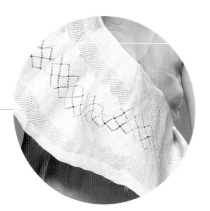

745

746

ION FIZ
SPAIN

AILANTO
SPAIN

747

748

ELISA PALOMINO
SPAIN

ION FIZ
SPAIN

749

750

DIANA DORADO
COLOMBIA

EWA I WALLA
SWEDEN

751

752

G.V.G.V.
JAPAN

MARTIN LAMOTHE
SPAIN

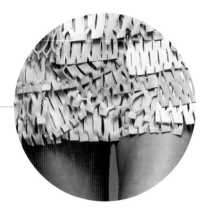

753

754

G.V.G.V.
JAPAN

ERICA ZAIONTS
UKRAINE

755

756

AILANTO
SPAIN

TSUMORI CHISATO
JAPAN

757

758

HARRIHALIM
INDONESIA

ANA LOCKING
SPAIN

759

760

IDA SJÖSTEDT
SWEDEN

© Kristian Löveborg

209

MALAFACHA BRAND
MEXICO

761

762

CARLOS DÍEZ
SPAIN

MANISH ARORA
INDIA

763

764

CATI SERRÀ
SPAIN

MARTIN LAMOTHE
SPAIN

765

766

CATI SERRÀ
SPAIN

DIANA DORADO
COLOMBIA

767

768

ELENA PRZHONSKAYA
UKRAINE

ELISA PALOMINO
SPAIN

769

770

DIANA DORADO
COLOMBIA

IDA SJÖSTEDT
SWEDEN

771

772

EWA I WALLA
SWEDEN

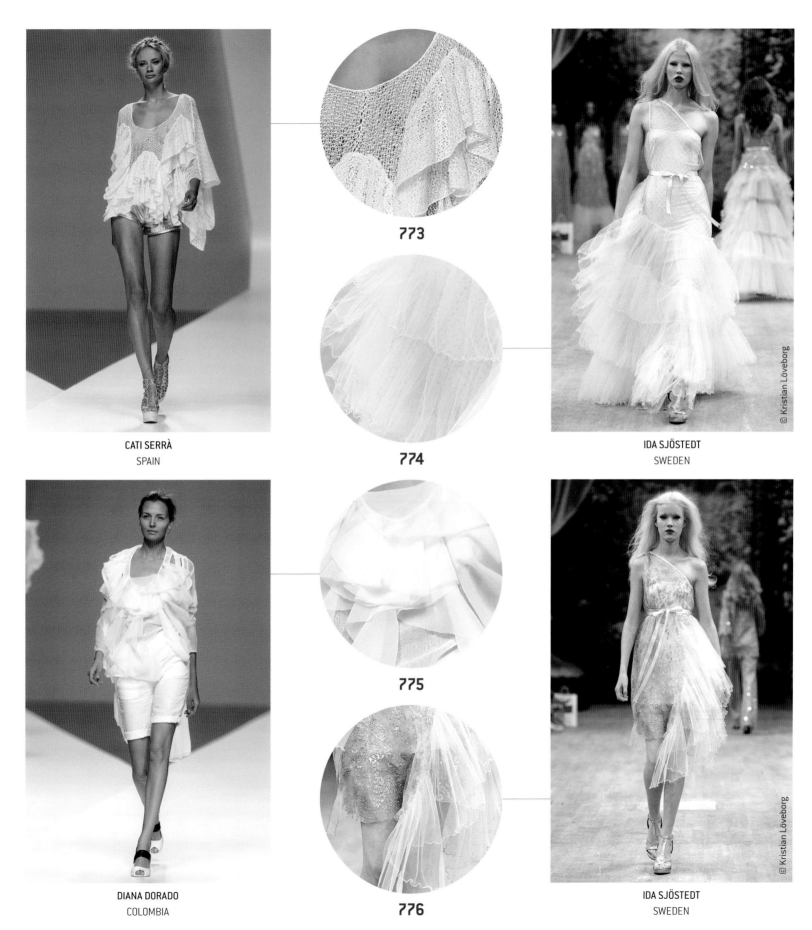

CATI SERRÀ
SPAIN

773

774

IDA SJÖSTEDT
SWEDEN

© Kristian Löveborg

DIANA DORADO
COLOMBIA

775

776

IDA SJÖSTEDT
SWEDEN

© Kristian Löveborg

213

RICARDO DOURADO
PORTUGAL

777

778

DIANA DORADO
COLOMBIA

© Kristian Löveborg

IDA SJÖSTEDT
SWEDEN

779

780

DIANA DORADO
COLOMBIA

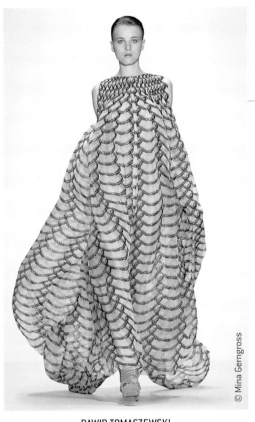

DAWID TOMASZEWSKI
POLAND

781

782

CAMILLA NORRBACK
FINLAND

EWA I WALLA
SWEDEN

783

784

VASSILIOS KOSTETSOS
GREECE

215

DAWID TOMASZEWSKI
POLAND

© Mina Gerngross

785

786

MALAFACHA BRAND
MEXICO

DAWID TOMASZEWSKI
POLAND

© Mina Gerngross

787

788

ELISA PALOMINO
SPAIN

216

GEORGIA HARDINGE
UK

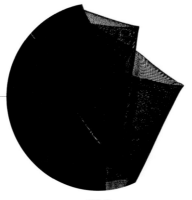

789

790

ERICA ZAIONTS
UKRAINE

© Kristian Löveborg

CAMILLA NORRBACK
FINLAND

791

792

BORA AKSU
TURKEY

TSUMORI CHISATO

JAPAN

793

794

ELISA PALOMINO

SPAIN

HARRIHALIM

INDONESIA

795

796

TSUMORI CHISATO

JAPAN

IDA SJÖSTEDT
SWEDEN

797

798

EWA I WALLA
SWEDEN

MAYA HANSEN
SPAIN

799

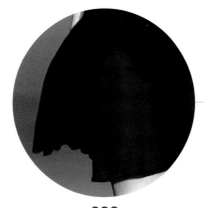

800

ELISA PALOMINO
SPAIN

© Kristian Löveborg

DECORATIVE APPLIQUÉS

DEKORATIVE APPLIKATIONEN

APLICACIONES DECORATIVAS

Decorative appliqués offer a wide range of possibilities. By adding the perfect piece, many designers covert a garment into a must of the season. International runways are brimming with studs, sequins, feathers, rhinestones, beads, ribbons, strings, fringes, tassels, braids, paintings and many more accessories in this fantasy world. In this chapter we will see elements like military-inspired epaulettes, satin ribbons and Baroque-style beaded corsets, or fragile items such as Swarovski crystals, which can be seen in the Canadian designer Mark Fast's latest collection, featured at London Fashion Week. Trends revive elements such as feathers, new concepts such as a long artificial hair or vinyl applications, wires, etc. as well as craftwork such as painting done by hand, complemented with other decorative motifs. Tradition and ethnic resources will also be a recurring feature in the proposals.

Wenn wir von dekorativen Applikationen sprechen, eröffnet sich ein breiter Fächer an Möglichkeiten, mit denen viele Designer in der Lage sind, das perfekte Stück zu applizieren, das ein Kleid in ein „Must" der Saison verwandelt. Drahtstifte, Pailletten, Federn, Edelsteine, Glasperlen, Bänder, Ketten, Fransen, Quasten, Tressen, Bemalungen und vieles, vieles mehr bilden dieses Universum der Fantasie, das die Laufstege der Welt erfüllt. In diesem Kapitel sehen wir Elemente wie militärisch inspirierte Epauletten, Satinbänder und Glasperlen als Verschlüsse von Korsetts, die des Barocks würdig wären, oder so zarte Elemente wie Swarovski-Kristalle, wie sie in der neuesten Kollektion des kanadischen Designers Mark Fast auf der London Fashion Week gezeigt wurden. Die aktuellen Trends lassen Elemente wie die omnipräsenten Federn wieder aufleben, neue Konzepte wie große Mengen künstlichen Haars oder Applikationen in Vinyl, Metallfäden usw., sowie echte Handwerkskunst, wie Handmalereien, die durch andere Schmuckelemente ergänzt werden. Auch Tradition und ethnische Ressourcen sind in den gezeigten Entwürfen eine Konstante.

Cuando hablamos de aplicaciones decorativas se abre un amplio abanico de posibilidades mediante el que muchos diseñadores tienen la habilidad de dar con la pieza perfecta que convierte una prenda en un *must* de la temporada. Tachuelas, lentejuelas, plumas, pedrería, abalorios, cintas, cadenas, flecos, borlas, galones, pinturas y un largo etcétera conforman este universo de fantasía que llena las pasarelas internacionales. En este capítulo veremos elementos como las charreteras de inspiración militar, cintas de raso y abalorios que rematan corsés dignos del Barroco; o elementos tan delicados como los cristales Swarovski, presentes en la última colección del diseñador canadiense Mark Fast, que exhibió en la London Fashion Week. Las tendencias reviven elementos como las omnipresentes plumas; nuevos conceptos, como un extenso pelo artificial o las aplicaciones en vinilo, hilos metálicos, etc; así como verdaderas artesanías, como las pinturas hechas a mano, complementadas con otros motivos ornamentales. La tradición y los recursos étnicos también serán una constante en las propuestas mostradas.

© Yannis Vlamos

MANISH ARORA

INDIA

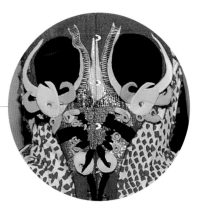

801

802

MALINI RAMANI

USA/INDIA

© Israel Esparza

MALAFACHA BRAND

MEXICO

803

804

MALINI RAMANI

USA/INDIA

MANISH ARORA
INDIA

805

806

AMERICAN PÉREZ
SPAIN

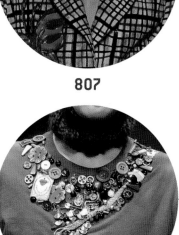

807

808

TSUMORI CHISATO
JAPAN

MALAFACHA BRAND
MEXICO

MARK FAST
CANADA

809

810

VICTORIO & LUCCHINO
SPAIN

AMERICAN PÉREZ
SPAIN

811

812

MALAFACHA BRAND
MEXICO

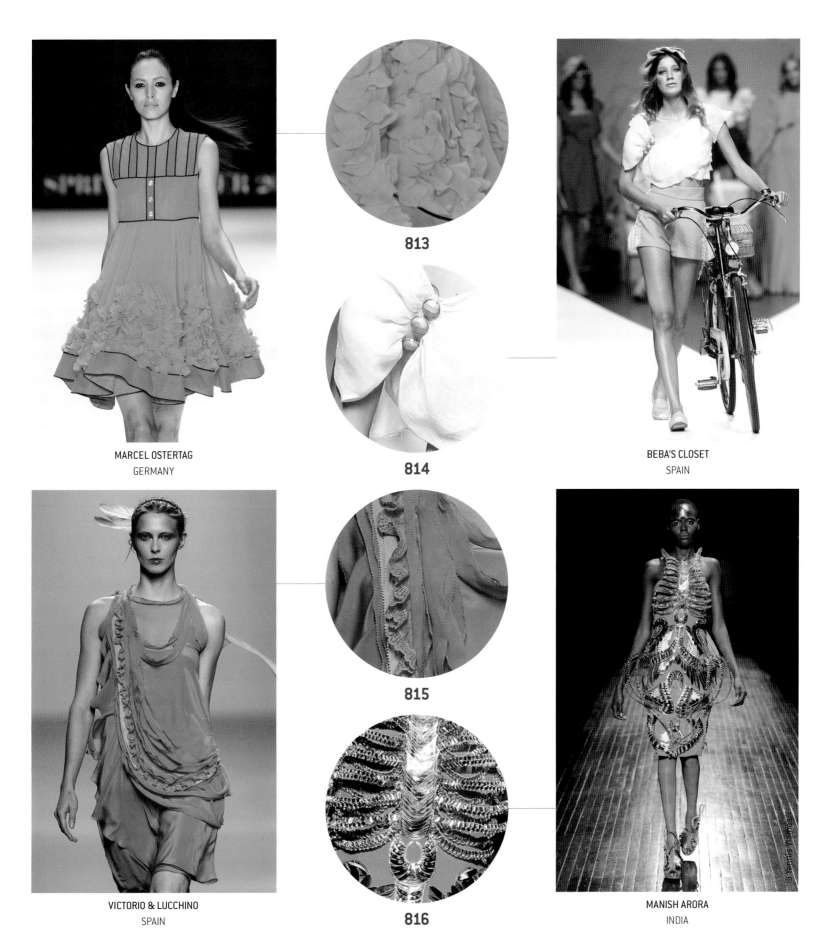

MARCEL OSTERTAG
GERMANY

813

814

BEBA'S CLOSET
SPAIN

VICTORIO & LUCCHINO
SPAIN

815

816

MANISH ARORA
INDIA

G.V.G.V.
JAPAN

817

818

EK THONGPRASERT
THAILAND

TSUMORI CHISATO
JAPAN

819

820

IDA SJÖSTEDT
SWEDEN

© Kristian Löveborg

SINPATRON
SPAIN

821

822

DESIGNSKOLEN KOLDING
DENMARK

MALAFACHA BRAND
MEXICO

823

824

TSUMORI CHISATO
JAPAN

227

825

ANJARA
SPAIN

826

DESIGNSKOLEN KOLDING
DENMARK

827

BIBIAN BLUE
SPAIN

828

G.V.G.V.
JAPAN

BIBIAN BLUE
SPAIN

829

830

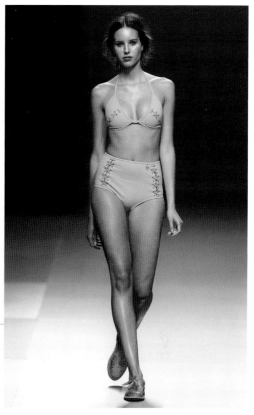

ANTONIO ALVARADO
SPAIN

MALAFACHA BRAND
MEXICO

831

832

TSUMORI CHISATO
JAPAN

229

EK THONGPRASERT
THAILAND

833

834

BIBIAN BLUE
SPAIN

TSUMORI CHISATO
JAPAN

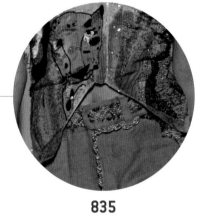

835

836

MALAFACHA BRAND
MEXICO

© Israel Esparza

MANISH ARORA
INDIA

837

838

BEBA'S CLOSET
SPAIN

MANISH ARORA
INDIA

839

840

BEBA'S CLOSET
SPAIN

MARK FAST
CANADA

841

MANISH ARORA
INDIA

842

AILANTO
SPAIN

843

844

MALAFACHA BRAND
MEXICO

VICTORIO & LUCCHINO
SPAIN

845

846

MANISH ARORA
INDIA

DIANA DORADO
COLOMBIA

847

848

BEBA'S CLOSET
SPAIN

233

MANISH ARORA
INDIA

849

850

ION FIZ
SPAIN

MARK FAST
CANADA

851

852

STAS LOPATKIN
RUSSIA

CATI SERRÀ
SPAIN

853

854

IDA SJÖSTEDT
SWEDEN

MAYA HANSEN
SPAIN

855

856

TSUMORI CHISATO
JAPAN

235

AMERICAN PÉREZ
SPAIN

857

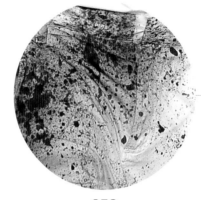

858

© Patrice Stable

KRIS VAN ASSCHE
BELGIUM

AMERICAN PÉREZ
SPAIN

859

860

SINPATRON
SPAIN

RICARDO DOURADO
PORTUGAL

861

862

STAS LOPATKIN
RUSSIA

STAS LOPATKIN
RUSSIA

863

864

ELISA PALOMINO
SPAIN

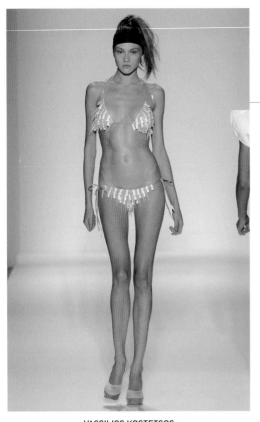

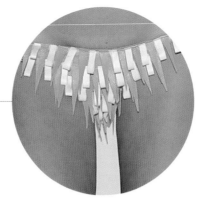

865

866

VASSILIOS KOSTETSOS
GREECE

EK THONGPRASERT
THAILAND

867

868

GEORGIA HARDINGE
UK

ALI CHARISMA
INDONESIA

DESIGNSKOLEN KOLDING
DENMARK

869

870

ALI CHARISMA
INDONESIA

DAWID TOMASZEWSKI
POLAND

871

872

QASIMI
UNITED ARAB EMIRATES

RICARDO DOURADO
PORTUGAL

873

874

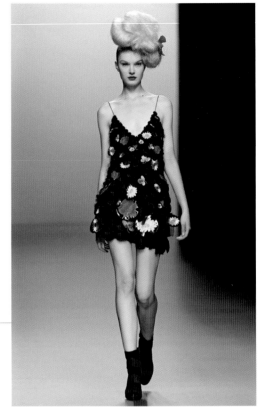

ELISA PALOMINO
SPAIN

VLADISLAV AKSENOV
RUSSIA

875

876

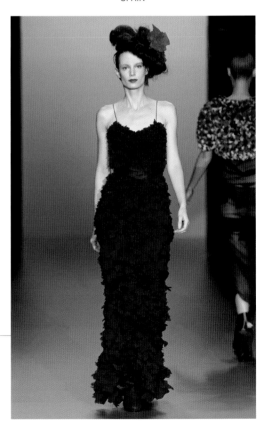

ELISA PALOMINO
SPAIN

VLADISLAV AKSENOV
RUSSIA

877

878

VASSILIOS KOSTETSOS
GREECE

MAYA HANSEN
SPAIN

879

880

MAL-AIMÉE
FRANCE

© Sébastien Agnetti

HARRIHALIM
INDONESIA

881

882

J JS LEE
KOREA

TIM VAN STEENBERGEN
BELGIUM

883

884

BIBIAN BLUE
SPAIN

ELISA PALOMINO
SPAIN

885

886

MARK FAST
CANADA

TSUMORI CHISATO
JAPAN

887

888

HARRIHALIM
INDONESIA

HARRIHALIM
INDONESIA

889

890

TSUMORI CHISATO
JAPAN

DESIGNSKOLEN KOLDING
DENMARK

891

892

DIMITRI
ITALY

IDA SJÖSTEDT
SWEDEN

893

894

ALI CHARISMA
INDONESIA

AMERICAN PÉREZ
SPAIN

895

896

DIMITRI
ITALY

ASHER LEVINE
USA

897

898

BIBIAN BLUE
SPAIN

ELISA PALOMINO
SPAIN

899

900

ASGER JUEL LARSEN
DENMARK

MARTIN LAMOTHE
SPAIN

901

902

ASHER LEVINE
USA

HARRIHALIM
INDONESIA

903

904

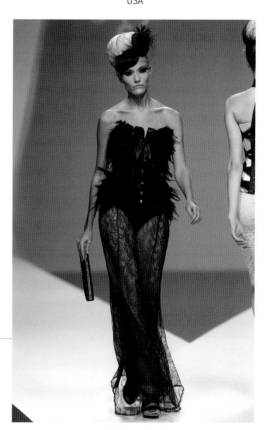

MAYA HANSEN
SPAIN

SEWING DETAILS

DETAILS BEI NÄHTEN UND SÄUMEN

DETALLES DE COSTURA

In this last chapter we will focus on the sewing details, which at times are sometimes less visible, but no less important or significant when appreciating a garment. On the one hand, we will study pure sewing elements such as bust and hip darts and French seams, used in transparent garments, etc. This chapter includes all those elements that have traditionally been used to sculpt the silhouette and add the finishing touches to garments, and now play an important role in the deconstructed garment, in volumes, architectural forms and asymmetries that are such a prominent feature in modern design. Lace edging, blond lace or yokes complete this section and, naturally, different styles of embroidery depending on the type of knot used in the work. This chapter also highlights the appliqué work, which is embroidered separately and then superimposed on the garment. It represents a fusion of details from the finest ateliers and the hardest working hands.

Für dieses letzte Kapitel sparen wir uns die Details der Näherei auf, die mitunter am wenigsten wahrnehmbar, jedoch bei der Bewertung eines Kleides nicht minder wichtig oder bedeutsam sind. Auf der einen Seite zeigen wir reine Nähelemente, wie Abnäher an Brust und Taille oder Nähereien wie die französische, die auf transparente Kleider appliziert sind usw. All diese Elemente, die traditionell zum Modellieren der Silhouette und zum Abschluss von Kleidern verwendet werden, spielen heute eine wichtige Rolle bei der Konfektion von dekonstruierten Kleidern, beim Volumen, architektonischen Formen und Asymmetrien, die in den avantgardistischsten Designs so präsent sind. Spitzen und Passen vervollständigen diesen Abschnitt und natürlich die Stickereien verschiedener Art aus dem Blickwinkel der angewandten Nähtechniken. Am Relief sehen wir, dass die Spitzenapplikationen eine besondere Rolle spielen, die einzeln gestickt und nachträglich auf ein Stück aufgebracht werden. Eine Potpourri von Details der exquisitesten Schneider und der geschicktesten Hände.

Hemos dejado para el último capítulo los detalles de costura, que en ocasiones son los menos perceptibles pero no por ello son menos importantes ni significativos a la hora de valorar una prenda. Mostraremos elementos puramente de costura, como las pinzas en busto y cadera, costuras como la francesa, aplicadas en prendas transparentes, etc. Todos ellos, elementos que tradicionalmente se han usado para modelar la silueta y rematar las prendas y que hoy juegan un papel importante en la confección de prendas deconstruidas, en los volúmenes, formas arquitectónicas y asimetrías que tan presentes están en el diseño más vanguardista. Puntillas, blondas o canesús completan este apartado junto a, como no, los bordados de diferentes tipos según el punto de costura empleado en la labor. Según el relieve, veremos que destacan los bordados de aplicación, que se bordan separadamente para después superponerlos a la prenda. Una amalgama de detalles procedentes de los talleres más exquisitos y las manos más laboriosas.

CATI SERRÀ
SPAIN

905

906

THE SWEDISH SCHOOL OF TEXTILES
SWEDEN

ELISA PALOMINO
SPAIN

907

908

ELISA PALOMINO
SPAIN

THE SWEDISH SCHOOL OF TEXTILES
SWEDEN

© Kristian Löveborg

909

910

ELISA PALOMINO
SPAIN

ANA LOCKING
SPAIN

911

912

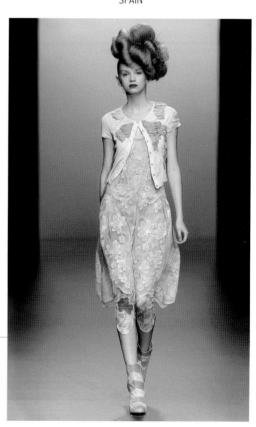

ELISA PALOMINO
SPAIN

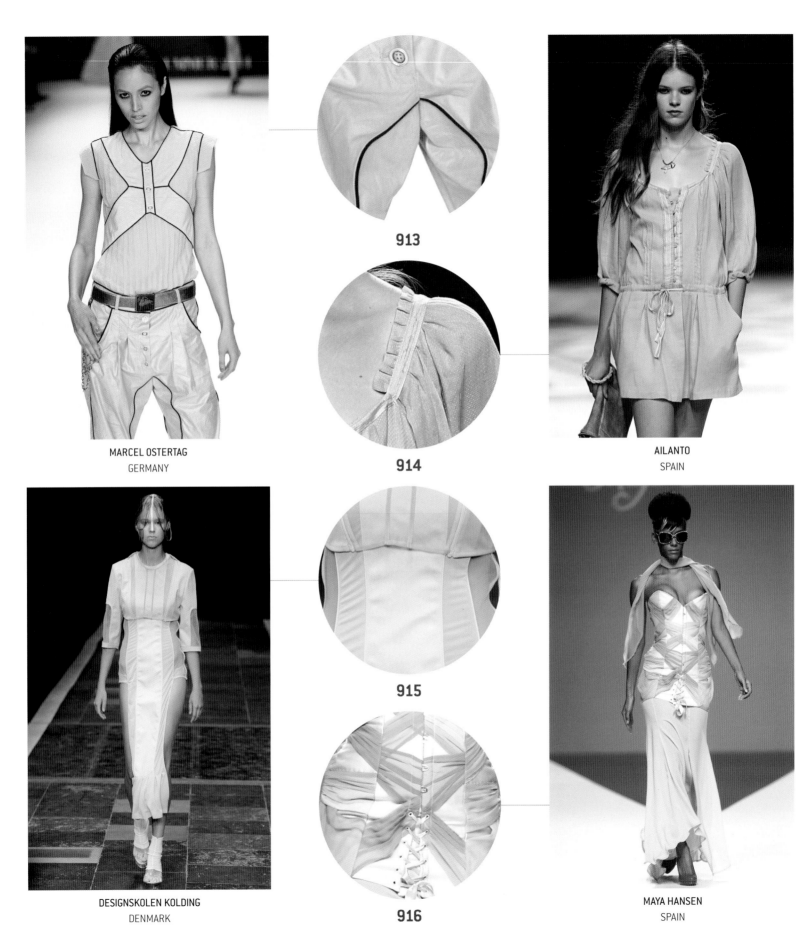

MARCEL OSTERTAG
GERMANY

913

914

AILANTO
SPAIN

DESIGNSKOLEN KOLDING
DENMARK

915

916

MAYA HANSEN
SPAIN

VASSILIOS KOSTETSOS
GREECE

917

918

ADA ZANDITON
UK

MARTIN LAMOTHE
SPAIN

919

920

ALI CHARISMA
INDONESIA

A.F. VANDEVORST
BELGIUM

921

922

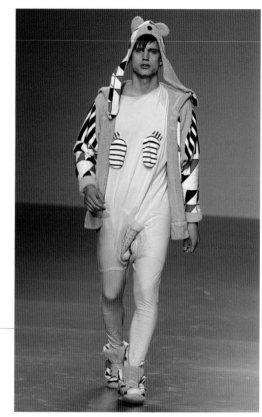

MARTA MONTOTO
SPAIN

KARLOTA LASPALAS
SPAIN

923

924

AILANTO
SPAIN

A.F. VANDEVORST
BELGIUM

925

926

MARTIN LAMOTHE
SPAIN

ELENA PRZHONSKAYA
UKRAINE

927

928

MARTIN LAMOTHE
SPAIN

ION FIZ
SPAIN

929

930

DESIGNSKOLEN KOLDING
DENMARK

BOHENTO
SPAIN

931

932

A.F. VANDEVORST
BELGIUM

STAS LOPATKIN
RUSSIA

933

934

THE SWEDISH SCHOOL OF TEXTILES
SWEDEN

© Kristian Löveborg

DIMITRI
ITALY

935

936

AILANTO
SPAIN

257

937

938

ANJARA
SPAIN

JULIUS
JAPAN

© Étienne Tordoir

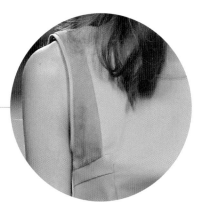

939

940

BOHENTO
SPAIN

THE SWEDISH SCHOOL OF TEXTILES
SWEDEN

© Kristian Löveborg

ERICA ZAIONTS
UKRAINE

941

942

© Sébastien Agnetti

MAL-AIMÉE
FRANCE

DESIGNSKOLEN KOLDING
DENMARK

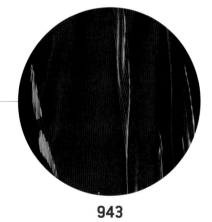

943

944

DESIGNSKOLEN KOLDING
DENMARK

945

HARRIHALIM

INDONESIA

946

VASSILIOS KOSTETSOS

GREECE

947

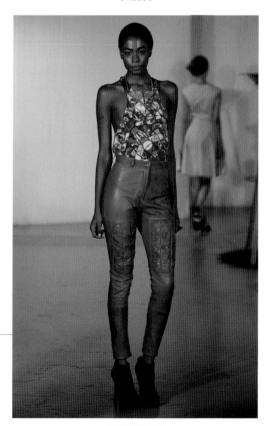

MANISH ARORA

INDIA

948

ADA ZANDITON

UK

ANA LOCKING
SPAIN

949

950

MARTIN LAMOTHE
SPAIN

CRAIG LAWRENCE
UK

951

952

ION FIZ
SPAIN

953

ADA ZANDITON
UK

954

CRAIG LAWRENCE
UK

955

ANA LOCKING
SPAIN

956

CRAIG LAWRENCE
UK

BEBA'S CLOSET
SPAIN

957

958

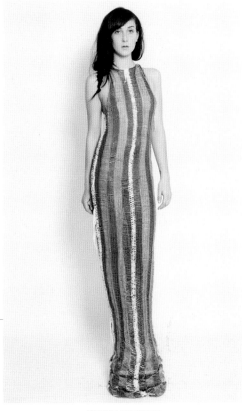

CRAIG LAWRENCE
UK

959

MARK FAST
CANADA

960

RICARDO DOURADO
PORTUGAL

CRAIG LAWRENCE
UK

961

962

MARK FAST
CANADA

IDA SJÖSTEDT
SWEDEN

© Kristian Löveborg

963

964

CRAIG LAWRENCE
UK

CARLOS DÍEZ
SPAIN

965

966

CRAIG LAWRENCE
UK

ION FIZ
SPAIN

967

968

JULIUS
JAPAN

© Étienne Jardoir

MARK FAST
CANADA

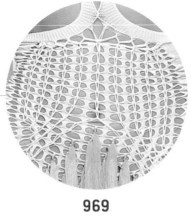

969

970

CARLOS DÍEZ
SPAIN

DESIGNSKOLEN KOLDING
DENMARK

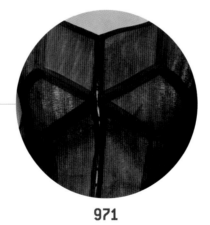

971

972

ELISA PALOMINO
SPAIN

THE SWEDISH SCHOOL OF TEXTILES
SWEDEN

973

974

THE SWEDISH SCHOOL OF TEXTILES
SWEDEN

DESIGNSKOLEN KOLDING
DENMARK

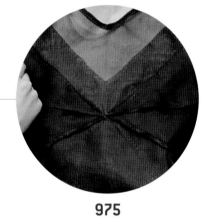

975

976

CAMILLA NORRBACK
FINLAND

© Kristian Löveborg

QASIMI

UNITED ARAB EMIRATES

977

978

ELENA SKAKUN

RUSSIA

VLADISLAV AKSENOV

RUSSIA

979

980

ALI CHARISMA

INDONESIA

VLADISLAV AKSENOV
RUSSIA

981

SPIJKERS EN SPIJKERS
THE NETHERLANDS

982

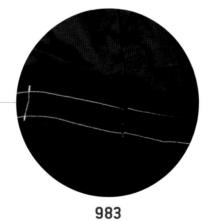

983

KRIS VAN ASSCHE
BELGIUM

© Patrice Stable

GEORGIA HARDINGE
UK

984

© Patrice Stable

KRIS VAN ASSCHE
BELGIUM

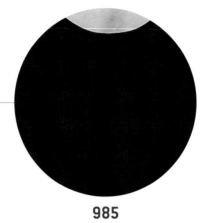

985

986

MARK FAST
CANADA

VLADISLAV AKSENOV
RUSSIA

987

988

SPIJKERS EN SPIJKERS
THE NETHERLANDS

DESIGNSKOLEN KOLDING
DENMARK

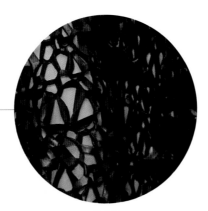

989

990

KRIS VAN ASSCHE
BELGIUM

© Patrice Stable

GEORGIA HARDINGE
UK

991

992

JULIUS
JAPAN

© Étienne Tordoir

DESIGNSKOLEN KOLDING
DENMARK

993

994

HARRIHALIM
INDONESIA

© Étienne Tordoir

JULIUS
JAPAN

995

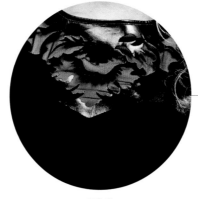

996

GEORGIA HARDINGE
UK

KRIS VAN ASSCHE
BELGIUM

997

998

BIBIAN BLUE
SPAIN

ELENA PRZHONSKAYA
UKRAINE

999

1000

QASIMI
UNITED ARAB EMIRATES

A.F. VANDEVORST / www.afvande vorst.be

An Vandevorst and Filip Arickx, A.F. Vandevorst, met in 1987 while studying at the Royal Academy of Fine Arts in Antwerp, Belgium. Later, An worked as chief assistant for Dries Van Noten and Filip worked as a freelance designer for fashion houses and as a stylist. In 1998, they joined forces to create a womenswear label, and since then they have presented their expressive collections bursting with personality in the Paris Fashion Week. They won the Venus Fashion Award for their debut on this runway.

An Vandervorst und Filip Arickx, A. F. Vandevorst, lernten sich 1987 während ihres Studiums an der Königlichen Kunsthochschule von Antwerpen kennen. Später arbeitete An als erste Assistentin von Dries Van Noten und Filip war freischaffend als Designer für Modehäuser und als Stylist tätig. 1998 vereinten sie ihre kreativen Geister um eine Damenmodefirma zu gründen und seitdem präsentieren sie ihre Kollektionen voller Emotionen und Persönlichkeit auf der Paris Fashion Week. Ihr Debüt auf diesem Laufsteg brachte ihnen den Preis „Vénus de la Mode" ein.

An Vandevorst y Filip Arickx, A.F. Vandevorst, se conocieron en 1987 cuando estudiaban en la Real Academia de Bellas Artes de Amberes. Más tarde, An trabajó como asistente principal de Dries Van Noten y Filip ejerció como diseñador *freelance* para casas de moda y como estilista. En 1998 unieron sus mentes creativas para crear una firma de moda femenina, y desde entonces presentan sus colecciones cargadas de emociones y personalidad en la Paris Fashion Week. Su debut en esta pasarela les valió el premio Venus de la Moda.

Ada Zanditon is a London-based designer who studied at the London College of Fashion, specializing in women's clothing. Throughout her career, she has worked in fashion houses such as Alexander McQueen, Jonathan Saunders and Gareth Pugh. She created her own company in 2008 with a distinctive ethnic flavor, and made her official runway debut at London Fashion Week, where she received rave reviews. She has also created costumes for musicians such as Patrick Wolf and celebrities such as Dita Von Teese and Lois Winstone are also fans of her label.

Ada Zanditon ist eine Londoner Designerin, die am London College of Fashion studierte, wo sie sich auf Damenkleider spezialisierte und in diesem Fach ihr Diplom erwarb. Während ihrer Laufbahn hat sie für Modefirmen wie Alexander McQueen, Jonathan Saunders oder Gareth Pugh gearbeitet. Ihr eigenes Unternehmen mit dem unterscheidenden ethnischen Touch gründete sie 2008 und gab ihr öffentliches Debüt mit einer Präsentation auf der London Fashion Week, wo sie sehr gute Kritiken bekam. Außerdem entwarf sie Kostüme für Musiker wie Patrick Wolf und auch Celebrities, wie Dita Von Teese und Lois Winstone, strahlen in ihren Kleidern.

Ada Zanditon es una diseñadora londinense que estudió en el London College of Fashion, graduándose en la especialidad de ropa femenina. A lo largo de su trayectoria ha trabajado en firmas de moda como Alexander McQueen, Jonathan Saunders o Gareth Pugh. Creó su firma en 2008 con un distintivo toque étnico, e hizo su presentación oficial en la London Fashion Week, donde que recogió muy buenas críticas. Además, ha diseñado vestuario para músicos como Patrick Wolf, y celebridades como Dita Von Teese y Lois Winstone también lucen su ropa.

ADA ZANDITON / www.adaz.co.uk

AGANOVICH / www.aganovich.com

Aganovich is the womenswear clothing label based in London designed by Nana Aganovich with narrative and conceptual influences devised by Brooke Taylor. Nana is a graduate of Dansk Designskole and an MA graduate of Central Saint Martins. Taylor is a former essayist and contributor for international literary and fashion magazines. With an impressive career and after having presented their collections at London Fashion Week, since 2009 Aganovich has shown their collections at Paris Fashion Week.

Das in London ansässige Damenmodeunternehmen Aganovich wurde durch die Designerin Nana Aganovich und Brooke Taylor gegründet, der die narrativen und konzeptuellen Einflüsse beiträgt. Nana studierte an der Dansk Designskole und belegte anschließend noch ein Masterstudium an der Londoner Central Saint Martins. Taylor ist Essayist und schreibt für Modemagazine. Mit einer makellosen Laufbahn und nach der Präsentation ihrer Kollektionen auf der London Fashion Week ist Aganovich seit 2009 im offiziellen Programm der Paris Fashion Week präsent.

Aganovich es la firma de ropa femenina afincada en Londres fundada por la diseñadora Nana Aganovich y Brooke Taylor, quien aporta las influencias narrativas y conceptuales. Nana se graduó en la Dansk Designskole y posteriormente realizó un máster en el Central Saint Martins. Taylor es ensayista literario y colaborador en revistas de moda. Con una trayectoria impecable y después de haber presentado sus colecciones en la London Fashion Week, Aganovich está presente, desde 2009, en el programa oficial de la Paris Fashion Week.

AILANTO / www.ailanto.com

Ailanto is the label created by the twin bothers Iñaki and Aitor Muñoz. Born in Bilbao, Spain, in 1968, the designers moved to Barcelona where they graduated in Fine Arts at the University of Barcelona UB. Iñaki complemented his studies with a degree in Fashion Design. The label's elegant collections are renowned for the geometric forms and artistic or cinematographic references. The collections have been sold internationally since 1995 with acclaimed runway presentations in Cibeles Madrid Fashion Week since 2001.

Die Firma Ailanto wurde durch die Zwillinge Iñaki und Aitor Muñoz gegründet. Die 1968 in Bilbao (Spanien) geborenen Designer zogen zum Kunststudium an der Universität von Barcelona um. Iñaki schloss sein Studium als Modedesigner ab. Ihre eleganten Kollektionen, geprägt durch geometrische Formen und künstlerische beziehungsweise kinematografische Referenzen, verkaufen sich im In- und Ausland seit 1995 und werden seit 2001 in jeder Saison auf der Cibeles Madrid Fashion Week gefeiert.

Ailanto es la firma creada por los gemelos Iñaki y Aitor Muñoz. Nacidos en Bilbao (España) en 1968, los diseñadores se trasladaron a la ciudad condal para estudiar Bellas Artes en la Universidad de Barcelona. Iñaki completó sus estudios graduándose en Diseño de Moda. Sus elegantes colecciones, caracterizadas por las formas geométricas y las referencias artísticas o cinematográficas, se venden dentro y fuera de nuestras fronteras desde 1995, y son aclamadas cada temporada en la Cibeles Madrid Fashion Week desde 2001.

The Russian designer Alena Akhmadullina is a Saint Petersburg Technology and Design Academy graduate. She presented her first prêt-à-porter collection at Paris Fashion Week in 2005 and since then she has presented a new collection on the French runway each season. In 2007, Alena opened an office in Moscow and the following year opened her first store in the center of the city. Alena Akhmadullina collections constitute a unique universe that combines Russian audacity with a Parisian sense of style.

Die russische Designerin Alena Akhmadullina studierte an der Universität für Technologie und Design St. Petersburg. Sie zeigte ihre erste Prêt-à-porter-Kollektion auf der Paris Fashion Week 2005 und ist seitdem in jeder Saison auf dem Laufsteg der französischen Hauptstadt vertreten. 2007 eröffnete sie eine Geschäftsstelle in Moskau und im Folgejahr ihren ersten Laden im Zentrum der Stadt. Die Kollektionen von Alena Akhmadullina bilden ein persönliches Universum ab, das russischen Wagemut mit dem Pariser Sinn für Stil verbindet.

La diseñadora rusa Alena Akhmadullina estudió en la Academia de Diseño y Tecnología de San Petersburgo. Mostró su primera colección de *prêt-à-porter* en la Paris Fashion Week en 2005, y desde entonces está presente en la pasarela de la capital francesa cada temporada. En 2007 abrió oficina en Moscú y al año siguiente inauguró su primera tienda en el centro de la ciudad. Las colecciones de Alena Akhmadullina conforman un universo personal que funde la audacia rusa y el sentido del estilo parisino.

ALENA AKHMADULLINA / www.alenaakhmadullina.com

ALI CHARISMA / www.alicharisma.com

Ali Charisma's label was created more than seven years ago, when he opened his first store in Seminyak, Indonesia. His design is characterized by the extreme opposition of color and texture. After achieving a balance between business and creativity, he began to show collections at Fashion Weeks in Bali, Jakarta, Hong Kong and Kuala Lumpur. His position in Bali as president of the Indonesian Fashion Designers Association allows him to actively participate in developing fashion in his country.

Die Firma von Ali Charisma entstand vor über sieben Jahren mit der Eröffnung seines ersten Ladens in Seminyak (Indonesien). Seine Designs sind geprägt durch den extremen Widerspruch zwischen Farbe und Textur. Nachdem er das Gleichgewicht zwischen Geschäft und Kreativität erlangt hatte, begann er seine Kollektionen auf den Modewochen von Bali, Jakarta, Hongkong und Kuala Lumpur zu zeigen. Sein Posten in Bali als Präsident der Indonesischen Vereinigung von Modeschöpfern erlaubt es ihm, aktiv an der Entwicklung der Mode seines Landes mitzuwirken.

La firma de Ali Charisma nació hace más de siete años, cuando abrió su primera tienda en Seminyak (Indonesia). Su diseño se caracteriza por la oposición extrema de color y textura. Después de alcanzar el equilibrio entre negocios y creatividad, comenzó a mostrar sus colecciones en las semanas de la moda de Bali, Yakarta, Hong Kong y Kuala Lumpur. Su posición en Bali como presidente de la Asociación Indonesia de Creadores de Moda le permite participar de forma activa en el desarrollo de la moda de su país.

AMERICAN PÉREZ / www.americanperez.es

American Pérez is the brainchild of Natalia Pérez and Jorge Bolado Moo. Natalia is a graduate of the ESDi School of Design in Barcelona and the University of Southampton; Jorge has a degree in Fine Arts from the University of Vigo and received an MA Styling degree from the Escola BAU in Barcelona. Together they created American Pérez in 2008, and have presented collections in Createurope Berlin and in El Ego de Cibeles, where they won the L'Oréal prize for the best fall/winter 2011 collection. They have also been finalists for the ModaFAD awards.

Hinter American Pérez stehen Natalia Pérez und Jorge Bolado Moo. Sie studierte an der Designhochschule ESDi in Barcelona und an der Universität von Southampton; er studierte Kunst an der Universität von Vigo und belegte ein Masterstudium in Stil an der Kunsthochschule der katalanischen Hauptstadt. Gemeinsam gründeten sie 2008 American Pérez und defilierten auf den Laufstegen von „Createurope Berlin" und „El Ego de Cibeles", wo sie den L'Oréal-Preis für die beste Herbst-Winter-Kollektion 2011 erhielten. Zudem gehörten sie zu den Finalisten der Modepreise FAD.

American Pérez está formada por Natalia Pérez y Jorge Bolado Moo. Ella se graduó en la Escuela Superior de Diseño ESDi de Barcelona y en la Universidad de Southampton; él es licenciado en Bellas Artes por la Universidad de Vigo y cursó un máster en Estilismo en la Escuela BAU de la capital catalana. Juntos crearon American Pérez en 2008, y han desfilado en Createurope Berlin y en El Ego de Cibeles, donde consiguieron el premio L'Oréal a la mejor colección otoño-invierno 2011. Además han sido finalistas de los premios ModaFAD.

ANA LOCKING / www.analocking.com

Ana González created Locking Shocking in 1996. For ten years, before the dissolution of the company, she received awards as the Prix de la moda Marie Claire for the best national designer in 2004. She founded her new label Ana Locking in 2008. Her debut collection won the L'Oréal Paris Award for the best collection from Cibeles Madrid Fashion Week. In 2009, she presented her collection in the New York Public Library during the NY Fashion Week and won the Cosmopolitan Award for the best designer of the year.

Ana González gründete Locking Shocking 1996. Zehn Jahre lang, bis zur Auflösung der Gesellschaft, erhielt sie Auszeichnungen wie den „Prix de la Mode Marie Claire" als beste nationale Designerin 2004. Ana Locking gründete sie 2008, deren Debütkollektion erhielt den Preis „L'Oréal Parìs" für die beste Kollektion auf der Cibeles Madrid Fashion Week. 2009 präsentierte sie im Rahmen der Modewoche der Stadt ihre Entwürfe in der Öffentlichen Bibliothek von New York und wurde von der Zeitschrift Cosmopolitan zur besten Designerin des Jahres gekürt.

Ana González creó Locking Shocking en 1996. Durante diez años, antes de la disolución de la sociedad, recibió galardones como el Prix de la Moda Marie Claire al mejor diseñador nacional de 2004. Fundó Ana Locking en 2008, cuya colección debut obtuvo el premio L'Oréal París a la mejor colección de la Cibeles Madrid Fashion Week. En 2009 presentó sus propuestas en la Biblioteca Pública de Nueva York dentro de la semana de la moda de la ciudad y fue premiada por la revista Cosmopolitan como mejor diseñadora del año.

ANJARA / www.anjara.com

Anjara García was born in Seville, Spain, and now resides in Shanghai, where she combines her role as a designer with her role as a DJ playing music in the best clubs. She studied Fashion Design at the Llotja School of Art and Design in Barcelona. In 2003, she opened her showroom in Seville and has since presented collection on runways such as Atmosphère in Paris, or SIMM, in Madrid, and in shows such as Bread & Butter Berlin or Who's next in Paris. In 2006, she opened her own store in Madrid and we can now see her proposals at Cibeles Madrid Fashion Week.

Anjara García wurde in Sevilla (Spanien) geboren und lebt derzeit in Schanghai, wo sie als Designerin und zugleich als DJ in den besten Clubs tätig ist. Sie studierte Modedesign an der Escuela Llotja de Arte y Diseño in Barcelona. 2003 eröffnete sie ihren Showroom in Sevilla und beteiligt sich seitdem an Schauen wie der „Atmosphère" in Paris oder „SIMM" in Madrid sowie an Messen, z.B. der „Bread & Butter" in Berlin oder dem Salon „Who's next" in Paris. 2006 eröffnete sie ihren eigenen Laden in Madrid und aktuell sehen wir ihre Entwürfe auf der Cibeles Madrid Fashion Week.

Anjara García nació en Sevilla (España) y ahora reside en Shanghái, donde combina su faceta de diseñadora con la de DJ de los mejores clubes. Estudió Diseño de Moda en la Escuela Llotja de Arte y Diseño de Barcelona. En 2003 abrió su showroom en Sevilla y desde entonces ha participado en pasarelas como Atmosphère, en París, o SIMM, en Madrid, y en ferias como la Bread & Butter de Berlín o el salón Who's next de París. En 2006 abrió su tienda propia en Madrid y actualmente vemos sus propuestas en la Cibeles Madrid Fashion Week.

ANNA MIMINOSHVILI / www.a-nic-o.com

The Russian designer Anna Miminoshvili inherited her talent from her parents who are architects. In her collections, she expresses her taste through architectural forms and elegant lines. Anna graduated from the A. N. Kosygin Moscow State Textile University, she then continued her studies at the University of Fashion in Lyon and the Academy of Design in Lodz, Poland. In 2010, she founded her own label, whose success has led her to show collections in the Russian Fashion Week and the Volvo-Moscow Fashion Week.

Die russische Designerin Anna Miminoshvili erbte das Talent von ihren Eltern, die Architekten sind. In ihren Kollektionen drückt sie ihren Geschmack durch den Symbolismus architektonischer Formen und die Eleganz der Linien aus. Anna studierte an der Moskauer Staatlichen Textiluniversität A. N. Kosygin und setzte anschließend ihre Ausbildung an der Modeuniversität von Lyon und der Designhochschule von Lodz (Polen) fort. 2010 gründete sie ihre eigene Marke, deren Erfolg sie auf die Laufstege der Russian Fashion Week und der Volvo-Moscow Fashion Week brachte.

La diseñadora rusa Anna Miminoshvili heredó el talento de sus padres, arquitectos. En sus colecciones expresa su gusto con el simbolismo de las formas arquitectónicas y la elegancia de las líneas. Anna se graduó en la Universidad Estatal del Textil A. N. Kosygin de Moscú, y después continuó su formación en la Universidad de la Moda de Lyon y en la Academia de Diseño de Lodz (Polonia). En 2010 fundó su propia marca, cuyo éxito la ha llevado a desfilar en la Russian Fashion Week y en la Volvo-Moscow Fashion Week.

ANTONIO ALVARADO / www.antonioalvarado.es

Antonio Alvarado from Alicante moved to Madrid in the eighties, where he revolutionized the way of presenting collections in clubs and designed costumes for movies such as those of Almodóvar. He has been a fixture at the Cibeles Madrid Fashion Week since 1984 and his collections, characterized by a meticulous pattern design and attention to detail, have appeared in the pages of the likes of Vanity Fair. For five years, he was the president of ModaFAD, a launching pad for young fashion designers.

Antonio Alvarado aus Alicante zog in den achtziger Jahren nach Madrid, wo er die Art der Präsentation von Kollektionen in Clubs revolutionierte und mit seinen Kreationen zu Filmen, unter anderem von Almodóvar, beitrug. Seit 1984 ist er auf der Cibeles Madrid Fashion Week präsent und seine Kollektionen, die sich durch akkurate Schnitte und Liebe zum Detail auszeichnen, sind auf der Titelseite von Vanity Fair erschienen. Fünf Jahre lang war er Präsident der ModaFAD, einer Vereinigung, die sich für junge Designer einsetzt.

El alicantino Antonio Alvarado se trasladó a Madrid en los ochenta, donde revolucionó la manera de presentar las colecciones en clubs y aportó sus creaciones a películas como las de Almodóvar. Ha estado presente en la Cibeles Madrid Fashion Week desde 1984, y sus colecciones, caracterizadas por un meticuloso patronaje y gusto por el detalle, han aparecido en cabeceras de la talla de Vanity Fair. Durante cinco años fue presidente de ModaFAD, una asociación que reivindica el espacio de los jóvenes diseñadores.

ASGER JUEL LARSEN / www.asgerjuellarsen.com

Since graduating with a BA menswear degree from London College of Fashion, the Danish designer Asger Juel Larsen has enjoyed a lot of media attention as well as being listed amongst the finalists at the prestigious Mittelmoda awards. His collections explore expressions of masculine strength marked by hard contrasts, such as stiff structures with delicate fabrics. This dichotomy is also reflected through futuristic materials such as leather, PVC, rubber cords and different types of metal.

Der dänische Designer Asier Juel Larsen genießt seit seinem Studium des Herrenmodedesigns am London College of Fashion enorme Medienaufmerksamkeit, zudem zählte er zu den Finalisten der angesehenen Mittelmoda-Preise. In seinen Kollektionen ergründet er die deutliche maskuline Kraft mit harten Kontrasten, wie scharfe Konturen mit zarten Geweben. Diese Dichotomie spiegelt sich auch in den futuristischen Materialien wie Leder, PVC, Gummischläuchen und verschiedenen Metallen wider.

Desde que se graduó en diseño de ropa masculina en el London College of Fashion, el diseñador danés Asger Juel Larsen ha gozado de una enorme atención de los medios, además de haber figurado entre los finalistas de los prestigiosos premios Mittelmoda. En sus colecciones explora la fuerza masculina marcada con duros contrastes, como estructuras rígidas con tejidos delicados. Esta dicotomía se refleja también a través de materiales futuristas como el cuero, el PVC, los cables de goma y diferentes tipos de metal.

ASHER LEVINE / www.asherlevine.com

Born in Florida, Asher developed a fascination with fashion from an early age. In 2006, he moved to New York, where he studied Managerial Entrepreneurship at Pace University. At the same time Asher began to independently create conceptual designs that could be seen on different personalities across the New York underground club circuit. With several menswear collections on the market, Asher defies fashion industry standards and the physical limitations of the garments.

Er wurde in Florida geboren und begeisterte sich schon in seiner Kindheit für Mode. In 2006 übersiedelte er nach New York, wo er an der Pace University Betriebswirtschaft studierte. Gleichzeitig begann er freiberuflich mit dem Entwurf experimenteller Designs, die schon bald von Persönlichkeiten der New Yorker Underground-Szene getragen wurden. Mit seinen verschiedenen Herrenkollektionen forderte Asher die Standards der Modebranche und die körperlichen Grenzen von Kleidung heraus.

Nacido en Florida, demostró su fascinación por la moda desde muy pequeño. En 2006 se trasladó a Nueva York, donde estudió Gestión de Empresas en la Pace University. Al mismo tiempo empezó a crear diseños experimentales de manera independiente, que pronto comenzaron a vestir diferentes figuras de la escena underground de Nueva York. Con varias colecciones masculinas en el mercado, Asher desafía los estándares de la industria de la moda y las limitaciones corporales de las prendas.

BEBA'S CLOSET / www. bebascloset.com

In 2002, the Spanish designer Belén Barbero decided to renounce her career as an economist and devote her time entirely to fashion. She studied at the Istituto Europeo di Design in Madrid, and in her last year she won the prize for best collection awarded by Burberry. After working for several labels, she opened her own atelier in Madrid in 2006 and since 2010 she has taken part in runways such as El Ego de Cibeles Madrid Fashion Week, with very fresh and feminine proposals. Currently she is working with the designer Miguel Palacio.

Im Jahr 2002 beschloss sie, ihre Karriere als Ökonomin aufzugeben und sich ganz der Mode zu widmen. Sie studierte am Istituto Europeo di Design in Madrid und in Abschlussjahr wurde sie mit dem Preis für die beste Kollektion ausgezeichnet, der von Burberry gestiftet wurde. Nachdem sie für verschiedene Unternehmen tätig war, eröffnete sie 2006 ihr Atelier in Madrid und nimmt seit 2010 mit sehr frischen, femininen Entwürfen an Modenschauen wie der El Ego de Cibeles auf der Madrid Fashion Week teil. Momentan arbeitet sie mit dem Designer Miguel Palacio zusammen.

En 2002, la española Belén Barbero decidió aparcar su carrera como economista y dedicarse plenamente a la moda. Estudió en el Istituto Europeo di Design, en Madrid, y en su último año obtuvo el premio a la mejor colección otorgado por Burberry. Después de trabajar para varias firmas, abrió su atelier en Madrid en 2006, y desde 2010 participa en pasarelas como El Ego de la Cibeles Madrid Fashion Week, con propuestas muy frescas y femeninas. Actualmente colabora con el diseñador Miguel Palacio.

BERNARD CHANDRAN / www.bernardchandran.com

At 16 he began studying Fashion Design in Petaling Jaya, Malaysia. After perfecting his technique in Paris, he returned home to open a small store in 1993, now a couture house, with very loyal followers. Awards such as the Look of the Year from the Open European Contest or Designer of the Year at the Malaysian International Fashion Awards support his successful career. He is also a major television personality as he has taken part in the reality show Project Runway Malaysia as a mentor.

Mit 16 Jahren begann er sein Studium des Modedesigns in Petaling Jaya (Malaysia). Nachdem er sein Handwerk in Paris perfektioniert hatte, kehrte er in sein Heimatland zurück, um dort 1993 ein kleines Geschäft zu eröffnen, das er in ein Schneideratelier mit treuer Gefolgschaft verwandelte. Preise wie der Look of the Year des Open European Contest oder die Auszeichnung zum Designer des Jahres bei den Malaysian International Fashion Awards sind ein Nachweis für seine erfolgreiche Karriere. Außerdem ist er in der Rolle des Mentors der Serie Reality Project Runway Malaysia eine wichtige TV-Persönlichkeit.

A los 16 años comenzó estudiando Diseño de Moda en Petaling Jaya (Malasia). Tras perfeccionar su técnica en París, regresó a su país para abrir una pequeña tienda en 1993, hoy convertida en casa de costura, con muy fieles seguidores. Premios como el Look of the Year del Open European Contest o el de Diseñador del Año, otorgado en los Malaysian International Fashion Awards, avalan su exitosa carrera. Además, es una importante figura televisiva por ejercer de mentor en el reality Project Runway Malaysia.

BIBIAN BLUE / www.bibianblue.com

Bibian Blue, a native of Barcelona trained as a graphic designer in the Escola Massana in her hometown, and subsequently graduated in a number of courses at the Academia Internacional de la Moda and postgraduates at FD Moda. She is an icon of vintage, retro and burlesque aesthetics, and the corset is her fetish garment. In 2000, she launched her first and successful collection, and now has points of sale throughout Europe, worldwide online distribution and boutique-atelier in the center of Barcelona.

Bibian Blue studierte Grafikdesign an der Escuela Massana in ihrer Heimatstadt Barcelona und setzte ihre Ausbildung mit Kursen an der Academia Internacional de Moda und einem Postgraduiertenstudium an der FD Moda fort. Ihr Stil erinnert an die vintage, retro und burlesque Ästhetik und das Korsett als Kleidungsstück hat die Funktion eines Fetisch. Im Jahr 2000 brachte sie ihre erste und sofort erfolgreiche Kollektion heraus. Heute verkaufen Einzelhändler in ganz Europa ihre Modelle, und ihre Mode ist sowohl online als auch in einem Boutique-Atelier im Zentrum Barcelonas erhältlich.

Bibian Blue estudió Diseño Gráfico en la Escuela Massana de Barcelona, su ciudad natal, y prosiguió su formación con cursos en la Academia Internacional de Moda y posgrados en FD Moda. Es todo un referente de la estética *vintage*, *retro* y *burlesque*, y el corsé es su prenda fetiche. En el año 2000 lanzó su primera y exitosa colección, y actualmente cuenta con puntos de venta en toda Europa, distribución mundial en línea y *boutique-atelier* en el centro de Barcelona.

BOHENTO / www.bohento.com

Cuca Ferrá studied Fashion Design, specializing in leather at the Centro Superior de Diseño de Moda in Madrid. Later, she worked for several fashion labels and furthered her studies in plastic arts. In 2008, together with her former partner Pablo de la Torre, she created Bohento. They present their very individual collections at the El Ego de Cibeles Madrid Fashion Week. Currently, Cuca is going solo at the forefront of Bohento and she is also a Fashion Design professor at the Polytechnic University of Madrid.

Cuca Ferrá studierte Modedesign mit Schwerpunkt Leder an der Modefachschule in Madrid. Später arbeitete er abwechselnd in verschiedenen Modefirmen und beendete sein Studium der Bildenden Kunst. In 2008 gründet er gemeinsam mit seinem ehemaligen Geschäftspartner Pablo de la Torre das Label Bohento und präsentiert seine extravaganten Kollektionen beim El Ego der El Ego de Cibeles Madrid Fashion Week. Moment ist Cuca der Chef von Bohento und als Design-Professor an der Polytechnischen Universität Madrid tätig.

Cuca Ferrá estudió Diseño de Moda en el Centro Superior de Diseño de Moda de Madrid, especializándose en piel. Más tarde, alternó su trabajo en varias firmas de moda con los estudios en artes plásticas. En 2008 crea Bohento junto con su exsocio Pablo de la Torre, y presenta sus colecciones, con un sello muy personal, en El Ego de la Cibeles Madrid Fashion Week. Actualmente Cuca está al frente de Bohento y además es profesora de Diseño de Moda en la Universidad Politécnica de Madrid.

BORA AKSU / www.boraaksu.com

London-based Turkish designer Bora Aksu graduated from Central Saint Martins. His graduation runway show won the sponsorship that prompted him to create his own brand, whose debut was with the fall/winter 2003 collection during London Fashion Week. The Guardian rated his runway presentation as "one of the top five shows in London." Since then, he has received the New Generation Award four times from the British Fashion Council.

Der Designer Bora Aksu ist türkischer Abstammung, lebt in London und studierte am Kunst- und Designcollege Central Saint Martins. Mit seiner Abschluss-Modenschau gewann er eine Auszeichnung, was ihn zur Gründung seiner eigenen Marke motivierte, die er zum ersten Mal mit der Herbst-Winterkollektion 2003 auf der London Fashion Week vorstellte. Die Zeitung The Guardian bewertete seine Präsentation auf dem Laufsteg als «eine der fünf besten Shows in London». Seitdem wurden sein tadellosen Kollektionen schon vier Mal vom British Fashion Council mit dem New Generation Award ausgezeichnet.

De origen turco y afincado en Londres, Bora Aksu se graduó en el Central Saint Martins. Con su desfile de graduación ganó el patrocinio que le impulsó a crear su propia marca, cuyo debut fue con la colección otoño-invierno 2003 durante la London Fashion Week. El periódico *The Guardian* valoró su presentación sobre la pasarela como «uno de los cinco mejores shows en Londres». Desde entonces, sus impecables colecciones han sido galardonadas en cuatro ocasiones por el Consejo Británico de la Moda con el New Generation Award.

CAMILLA NORRBACK / www.camillanorrback.com

At the age of 13 Camilla Norrback, born in Finland and now settled in Sweden, got her first sewing machine and since then she knew that she wanted to dedicate her life to fashion. Camilla Norrback is a well-known label in Sweden and has been nominated for major fashion awards. Since 2002, Camilla has been committed to creating ecologically sustainable garments called Ecoluxury. In addition to her female collection that she presents at the Stockholm Fashion Week, in 2010 she created the male line Norrback.

Camilla Norrback wurde in Finnland geboren und lebt in Schweden. Mit 13 Jahren bekam sie ihre erste Nähmaschine – dann wusste sie, dass sie ihr Leben der Mode widmen wollte. Camilla Norrback ist eine in Schweden sehr bekannte Marke und wurde für wichtige Modepreise nominiert. Mit ökologischem Engagement entwirft Camilla seit 2002 umweltbewusste Mode, die sie als Ecoluxury bezeichnet. Neben ihrer Damenkollektion, die sie auf der Stockholm Fashion Week präsentiert, gründete sie 2010 ihre Herrenlinie Norrback.

Camilla Norrback, nacida en Finlandia y afincada en Suecia, tuvo su primera máquina de coser a los 13 años: entonces supo que quería dedicar su vida a la moda. Camilla Norrback es una firma bien conocida en Suecia, y ha sido nominada a importantes premios de moda. Concienciada con el medio ambiente, desde 2002 Camilla diseña prendas ecológicas que denomina Ecoluxury. Además de su línea femenina, que se presenta en la Stockholm Fashion Week, en 2010 creó la línea masculina Norrback.

CARLOS DÍEZ / www.myspace.com/diezdiez

Carlos Díez Díez was born in Bilbao, Spain, but moved to Madrid, where he now has his studio-atelier. His style is totally creative and original. He has worked for designers such as Antonio Alvarado, and since 2006 he has created a sportswear collection each season for the American label Converse. In 2004, he began to showcase his collections at the Cibeles Madrid Fashion Week, where in 2006 he won the L'Oréal award for the best collection. In 2009 he opened his first store in the Spanish capital.

Carlos Díez Díez wurde in Bilbao (Spanien) geboren und lebt in Madrid, wo er heute sein Atelier hat. Sein Stil ist absolut kreativ und originell. Er arbeitete mit Designern wie Antonio Alvarado zusammen, und seit 2006 entwirft er für die Firma Converse eine Sportkollektion. Im Jahr 2004 zeigte er sein Können bei der Modenschau Cibeles der Madrid Fashion Week, wo er 2006 den L'Oréal-Preis für die beste Kollektion erhielt. Seinen ersten Laden eröffnete er 2009 in der spanischen Hauptstadt.

Carlos Díez Díez nació en Bilbao (España) pero se trasladó a Madrid, donde ahora tiene su estudio-taller. Su estilo es absolutamente creativo y original. Ha colaborado para diseñadores como Antonio Alvarado, y desde 2006 crea una colección sport por temporada para la firma americana Converse. En 2004 comenzó a mostrar sus propuestas en la Cibeles Madrid Fashion Week, donde obtuvo en 2006 el premio L'Oréal a la mejor colección. En 2009 abrió su primera tienda en la capital española.

CATI SERRÀ / www.catiserra.com

Cati Serrà was born in Majorca, Spain. She is a graduate from the ESDi School of Design in Barcelona, receiving the Gold Medal for the best student in her class. She has carried out internships with labels such as Miguel Adrover. In 2008, she worked alongside him for the presentation of his collection at New York Fashion Week. That same year she founded her menswear and womenswear label, pigeonholed for its comfort, elegance, and careful design. She shows her collections on runways such as El Ego de Cibeles Madrid Fashion Week.

Cati Serrà wurde auf der spanischen Insel Mallorca geboren. Ihren Abschluss machte sie an der Escuela Superior de Diseño ESDi in Barcelona mit der Goldmedaille für den besten Schüler ihres Abschlussjahrgangs. Sie absolvierte Praktika bei verschiedenen Marken, darunter Miguel Adrover, mit dem sie 2008 an der Vorstellung seiner Kollektion im Rahmen der New York Fashion Week zusammenarbeitete. Im gleichen Jahr gründete sie ihre Modemarke für Damen und Herren, die sich durch Bequemlichkeit, Eleganz und Detailgenauigkeit auszeichnet. Zu sehen ist ihre Kollektion unter anderem bei der Modenschau El Ego de Cibeles der Madrid Fashion Week.

Cati Serrà nació en Mallorca (España). Se graduó en la Escuela Superior de Diseño ESDi de Barcelona, con la Medalla de Oro al mejor alumno de su promoción. Ha realizado prácticas en firmas como la del diseñador Miguel Adrover, con quien en 2008 trabajó para la presentación de su colección en la New York Fashion Week. Ese mismo año fundó su firma para hombre y mujer, caracterizada por ser cómoda, elegante y estudiada, y cuyas propuestas se muestran en pasarelas como El Ego de la Cibeles Madrid Fashion Week.

CHARLIE LE MINDU / www.charlielemindu.com

Charlie Le Mindu was born in France. He was a hairdressing prodigy during his time at the French Hair Academy. Then he went from the academic discipline to becoming a fashion stylist in Berlin, a true master of haute-coiffure. In 2009, he wowed with his first fashion collection at London Fashion Week, with an immediate response from magazines around the world, such as *Vogue Italia*, *Vogue Hommes Japon* and *i-D*. He currently is the star of a successful show on KonbiniTV, *Charlie's Treatment*.

Charlie Le Mindu wurde in Frankreich geboren. An der French Hair Academy war er bereits ein angesehener Coiffeur. Von der akademischen Arbeit wechselte er zur Tätigkeit eines Modestylisten in Berlin –er ist ein Meister der Haute-Coiffure. Im Jahr 2009 überraschte er auf der London Fashion Week mit seiner ersten Modekollektion – und sofort fand er Anklang bei Modezeitschriften weltweit, darunter Vogue Italia, Vogue Hommes Japan o i-D. Momentan hat er ein erfolgreiches Programm auf KonbiniTV mit dem Titel Charlie's Treatment.

Charlie Le Mindu nació en Francia. Era un prodigio de la peluquería ya en la French Hair Academy. Pasó de la disciplina académica a ser un estilista de moda en Berlín, un auténtico maestro del *haute-coiffure*. En 2009 sorprendió con su primera colección de moda en la London Fashion Week, con una respuesta inmediata de las revistas de todo el mundo, como Vogue Italia, Vogue Hommes Japon o i-D. Actualmente tiene un exitoso programa en KonbiniTV, *Charlie's Treatment*.

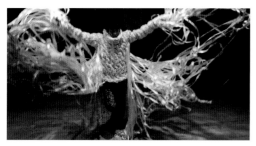

CRAIG LAWRENCE / www.craiglawrence.co.uk

Craig Lawrence is a knitwear designer, born in Ipswich, United Kingdom, and based in London. He graduated from Central Saint Martins. Over six seasons, he produced knitwear for Gareth Pugh, before establishing his own label. With his debut at London Fashion Week, Craig was awarded the New Generation sponsorship by the British Fashion Council, a support he has had for four seasons. He has recently participated in London Show Rooms, the initiative that encourages the presence of young London designers in New York.

Der Designer Craig Lawrence stammt aus Ipswich im Vereinigten Königreich und lebt in London. Er ist Absolvent des Central Saint Martins. Vor der Gründung seines Labels produzierte er für die Dauer von sechs Saisons die Strickkollektionen von Gareth Pugh. Seit seinem Debüt auf der London Fashion Week wurde er für vier Saisons von der New Generation Sponsorship des British Fashion Council unterstützt. Seit kurzem beteiligt er sich an den London Show Rooms, einer Initiative zur Förderung junger Londoner Designer in New York.

El diseñador de punto Craig Lawrence, nacido en Ipswich (Reino Unido) y afincado en Londres, se graduó en el Central Saint Martins. Antes de crear su firma, produjo las colecciones de punto de Gareth Pugh durante seis temporadas. Con su debut en la London Fashion Week obtuvo el patrocinio New Generation del Consejo Británico de la Moda, con el que ha contado cuatro temporadas. Recientemente ha participado en London Show Rooms, la iniciativa que fomenta la presencia de los jóvenes diseñadores londinenses en Nueva York.

DAWID TOMASZEWSKI / www.dawid-tomaszewski.com

Dawid was born in Poland. He studied at the London College of Fashion and the Akademie der Künste in Berlin, having studied Art History at Poznan. During his studies, he worked for Sonia Rykiel and when he finished, he was in companies such as Reebok, in Boston, or Comme des Garçons, in Tokyo, until he founded his own label in 2009. Her first collection won the Young Designer Award at Berlin Fashion Week. Tomaszewski's proposals have been influenced by art, architecture and a passion for jazz.

David wurde in Polen geboren. Er studierte Modedesign am London College of Fashion und an der Akademie der Künste in Berlin. Er absolvierte das Studium in Kunstgeschichte an der University of Fine Arts in Posen. Während seines Studiums arbeitete er für Sonia Rykiel und nach Beendigung seiner Ausbildung war er für verschiedene Unternehmen wie Reebok in Boston oder Comme des Garçons in Tokio tätig. Seine erste Kollektion gewann den Young Designer Award der Berlin Fashion Week. Die Entwürfe von Tomaszewki sind inspiriert von Kunstgeschichte, Architektur und seiner Leidenschaft für Jazz.

Dawid nació en Polonia. Estudió en el London College of Fashion y en la Akademie der Künste de Berlín, después de haber cursado Historia del Arte en Poznan. Durante sus estudios trabajó para Sonia Rykiel y una vez finalizados pasó por empresas como Reebok, en Boston, o Comme des Garçons, en Tokio, hasta que fundó su propia marca en 2009. Su primera colección ganó el Young Designer Award en la Berlin Fashion Week. Las propuestas de Tomaszewki tienen influencias del arte, la arquitectura y la pasión por la música *jazz*.

DESIGNSKOLEN KOLDING / www.designskolenkolding.dk

Beate Godager, Anne Mette Kjærgaard Jensen, Mette Daring fashion & Mette Gliemann textile, Mette Marie Krarup Bertelsen, Linda Gunnarsson, Sidse Bordal, Siff Pristed Nielsen, Sophie Lassen, Lisbeth Grosen Nielsen, Alexandra Lindek, Betina Møller, Anja Merete Larsen.

Danish design represents a mark of quality and has a reputation that goes far beyond the borders of its country. The work of Designskolen Kolding helps to strengthen the position of Danish fashion design both nationally and internationally, training young designers who represent the forefront of Danish fashion and through interesting concepts and proposals. His collections, presented at the Copenhagen Fashion Week, stand out for their studied pattern design, impossible shapes and surprising details.

Dieses dänische Label zeichnet sich durch Qualität aus und ist bis weit hinaus über die Landesgrenzen bekannt. Die Arbeit der Designskolen hilft dabei,die Position des dänischen Designs sowohl auf nationaler wie auf internationaler Ebene zu stärken, denn es bildet junge Designer aus, die zur Avantgarde der dänischen Mode zählen und begeistert mit interessanten Konzepten und Entwürfen. Die Kollektionen, präsentiert auf der Copenhagen Fashion Week, zeichnen sich durch ihre wunderbare Schneiderkunst, extravaganten Formen und überraschenden Details aus.

El diseño danés representa una marca de calidad y tiene una reputación que va mucho más allá de las fronteras del país. La labor de la Designskolen Kolding ayuda a consolidar la posición del diseño danés tanto a nivel nacional como internacional, formando a jóvenes diseñadores que demuestran la vanguardia de la moda danesa a través de interesantes conceptos y propuestas. Sus colecciones, presentadas en la Copenhagen Fashion Week, destacan por su estudiado patronaje, las formas imposibles y los detalles sorprendentes.

DIANA DORADO / www.dianadorado.com

The Colombian designer Diana Dorado is based in Barcelona, where she studied Fashion Design at the ESDi School of Design. She has won the ModaFAD award for best designer and has participated in the 080 Barcelona Fashion, the Pasarela Abierta de Murcia and El Ego de Cibeles Madrid Fashion Week. Diana Dorado has earned herself a place among the great revelations of Spanish fashion with colorful, urban and very feminine proposals.

Die kolumbianische Designerin Diana Dorado lebt in Barcelona, wo sie an der Escuela Superior de Diseño (ESDi) Modedesign studierte. Premio ModaFAD für den besten Designer ausgezeichnet und nahm an der 080 Barcelona Fashion, der Pasarela Abierta de Murcia und der Modenschau El Ego de Cibeles Madrid Fashion Week teil. Diana Doradohat sich mit ihren bunten, urbanen und sehr femininen Entwürfen in der spanischen Modewelt einen Namen gemacht.

La diseñadora colombiana Diana Dorado está afincada en Barcelona, donde estudió Diseño de Moda en la Escuela Superior de Diseño ESDi. Ha conseguido el Premio ModaFAD al mejor diseñador y ha participado en la 080 Barcelona Fashion, la Pasarela Abierta de Murcia y El Ego de la Cibeles Madrid Fashion Week. Diana Dorado ha conseguido hacerse un hueco entre las grandes revelaciones de la moda española con propuestas coloristas, urbanas y muy femeninas.

DIMITRI BY DIMITRIOS PANAGIOTOPOULOS
www.bydimitri.com

The Greek-Italian designer Dimitri Panagiotopoulos from the South Tyrol studied at the famous fashion school ESMOD and later earned an MA in Fashion Design at the Istituto Marangoni in Milan. After working for prestigious labels like Jil Sander, Hugo Boss and Vivienne Westwood, he opened his first store in the center of Merano, Italy, and currently presents two annual collections of harmonic and feminine garments at the Mercedes-Benz Fashion Week Berlin.

Dimitri Panagiotopoulos ist griechisch-italienischer Herkunft und stammt aus Südtirol. Er studierte an der bekannten Modeschule ESMOD und machte seinen Master in Modedesign am Istituto Marangoni in Mailand. Nach einer Tätigkeit für namhafte Unternehmen wie Jil Sander, Hugo Boss und Vivienne Westwood eröffnete er sein erstes Geschäft in derInnenstadt von Meran (Italien) und momentan präsentiert er im Rahmen des offiziellen Programms der Mercedes-Benz Fashion Week Berlin jährlich Kollektionen in sehr harmonischem, femininem Stil.

Dimitri Panagiotopoulos, de orígenes griegos e italianos y procedente del Tirol del Sur, estudió en la famosa escuela de moda ESMOD y más tarde realizó un máster en Diseño de Moda en el Istituto Marangoni de Milán. Tras trabajar para prestigiosas firmas como Jil Sander, Hugo Boss y Vivienne Westwood, abrió su primera tienda en el centro de Merano (Italia) y actualmente presenta dos colecciones anuales, armónicas y muy femeninas, en el programa oficial de la Mercedes-Benz Fashion Week Berlin.

EK THONGPRASERT / www.ekthongprasert.be

Ek Thongprasert was born in Bangkok. After completing his first degree in Architecture, he attended one of the most famous fashion schools, the Royal Academy of Fine Arts in Antwerp, which has produced many famous designers. In 2008, he created his eponymous label with a strong conceptual approach, along with jewelry designer Noon Passama, whom he met during his first degree at the University of Chulalongkorn, one of the most prestigious in Thailand.

Ek Thongprasert wurde in Bangkok geboren. Nach seinem Abschluss in Architektur absolvierte er eine der berühmtesten Modeschulen, die Königliche Akademie der Schönen Künste von Antwerpen, die zahlreiche bekannte Absolventen hervorgebracht hat. In 2008 gründet er unter seinem Namen ein Modelabel mit ausgeprägtem konzeptuellem Ansatz, an dem auch die Schmuckdesignerin Noon Passama beteiligt ist, die er während seines Studiums an der Chulalongkorn-Universität kennenlernte, einer der berühmtesten Universitäten Thailands.

Ek Thongprasert nació en Bangkok. Una vez terminado su primer grado, en Arquitectura, se unió a una de las escuelas de moda más famosas, la Real Academia de Bellas Artes de Amberes, de la que han salido muchos diseñadores bien conocidos. En 2008 pone en marcha su firma epónima con un fuerte enfoque conceptual, junto con la diseñadora de joyas Noon Passama, a quien conoció durante su grado en la Universidad de Chulalongkorn, una de las más prestigiosas de Tailandia.

ELENA PRZHONSKAYA / www.przhonskaya.com

Elena Przhonskaya was born in Ukraine. She graduated from the Kyiv National University of Technology and Design in 2007. During her studies she won several competitions for young designers in Ukraine and Russia and participated in the national television project PROfashion. After graduating, she opened her own studio in the center of Kiev with the aim of developing a strong brand with an international vision. Since then Elena is a regular at the Ukrainian Fashion Week.

Elena Przhonskaya wurde in der Ukraine geboren. Im Jahr 2007 absolvierte sie die Staatliche Kiewer Universität für Technologie und Design. Während ihres Studiums gewann sie mehrere Wettbewerbe für junge Designer in der Ukraine und Russland und nahm am Projekt PROFashion des nationalen Fernsehens teil. Nach ihrem Abschluss eröffnete sie im Zentrum von Kiew ihr eigenes Studio mit dem Ziel, eine eigene Marke mit starker internationaler Prägung zu gründen. Seitdem nimmt Elena regelmäßig an der Ukrainian Fashion Week teil.

Elena Przhonskaya nació en Ucrania. Se graduó en la Universidad Nacional de Tecnología y Diseño de Kiev en 2007. Durante sus estudios ganó varios concursos de jóvenes diseñadores en Ucrania y Rusia y participó en el proyecto de la televisión nacional PROfashion. Tras su graduación abrió su propio estudio en el centro de Kiev, con el objetivo de desarrollar una marca fuerte con visión internacional. Desde entonces Elena participa regularmente en la Ukranian Fashion Week.

ELENA SKANKUN / naum_ann@bk.ru

The Russian designer Elena Skankun boasts an excellent track record. She has won competitions such as the Russian Silhouette in 2003 and has presented collections on international runways such as Roma Altamoda, thanks to an internship in the Saga Design Center of Saga Furs. She is also the director of the Khanty-Mansiysk International Fashion institution. Her collections present at the Moscow Fashion Week stand out for their elegance and mastery of her favorite materials, tulle and leather.

Die russische Designerin Elena Skankun hat bereits einige Erfolge vorzuweisen. Sie gewann Wettbewerbe wie im Jahr 2003 den Russian Silhouette und nahm an verschiedenen internationalen Modenschauen teil, darunter die Roma Altamoda, was ihr aufgrund eines Praktikums im Saga Design Center von Saga Furs gelang. Außerdem leitet sie das Internationale Zentrum für Mode in Khanty-Mansijsk. Ihre Kollektionen werden auf der Moscow Fashion Week gezeigt und begeistern durch Eleganz und den perfekten Umgang mit ihren Lieblingsmaterialien: Tüll und Leder.

La diseñadora rusa Elena Skankun puede presumir de una excelente trayectoria. Ha ganado concursos como el Russian Silhouette en 2003 y ha participado en pasarelas internacionales como Roma Altamoda, gracias a unas prácticas en el Saga Design Center de Saga Furs. Además, es la directora de la institución Centro Internacional de la Moda de Janti-Mansisk. Sus colecciones, presentes en la Moscow Fashion Week, destacan por su elegancia y el dominio de sus materiales predilectos: el tul y la piel.

ELISA PALOMINO / www.elisapalomino.com

This Valencian studied at Central Saint Martins in London. After several years working at Moschino, she moved to Paris. For eight years she was director of the John Galliano studio, while also working at the Christian Dior Haute Couture collection. After collaborating with Roberto Cavalli, in 2008 she moved to New York to become vice president of design for Diane von Furstenberg. In 2010, she created her own label and showed her collections in New York and Cibeles Madrid Fashion Weeks.

Elisa stammt aus Valencia und studierte am Central Saint Martins in London. Nachdem sie einige Jahre für Moschino gearbeitet hatte, zog sie nach Paris. Acht Jahre leitete sie das Studio von John Galliano und arbeitete währenddessen auch an den Couture-Kollektionen von Christian Dior. Nach einer Tätigkeit für Roberto Cavalli zog sie 2008 nach New York und wurde stellvertretende Chefdesignerin bei Diane von Fürstenberg. Im Jahr 2010 gründete sie ihr eigenes Label und zeigt ihre Kollektion auf der New York Fashion Week und bei der Cibeles Madrid.

Esta valenciana estudió en el Central Saint Martins de Londres. Tras varios años trabajando en Moschino, se mudó a París. Durante ocho años fue directora de estudio de John Galliano, mientras colaboraba en las colecciones de alta costura de Christian Dior. Después de pasar por Roberto Cavalli, en 2008 se mudó a Nueva York para convertirse en vicepresidenta de diseño de Diane von Furstenberg. En 2010 creó su propia firma, y desde entonces desfila en las semanas de la moda de Nueva York y Cibeles Madrid.

ERICA ZAIONTS / www.ericazaionts.com

The Ukrainian designer based in Moscow Erica Zaionts graduated from the A. N. Kosygin Moscow State Textile University. Her label is a family business founded in 2001 and among its main virtues is its self-made manufacturing. Erica is considered as one of the few Russian designers who creates top quality prêt-à-porter clothing. Her collections, shown at Moscow Fashion Week, are characterized by their powerful image and recognizable style that is based on the practicality of forms.

Die ukrainische Designerin Erica Zaionts lebt in Moskau und ist Absolventin der Staatlichen Textiluniversität A. N. Kossygin in Moskau. Ihr Label ist ein 2001 gegründetes Familienunternehmen, und ihr Markenzeichen ist die Eigenherstellung ihrer Entwürfe. Erica gilt als eine der russischen Designerinnen für Prêt-à-Porter höchster Qualität. Ihre Kollektionen werden auf der Moskow Fashion Week gezeigt und punkten mit ihrem Image der Entschlossenheit und einem Stil mit hohem Wiedererkennungswert, der auf der Praktikabilität ihrer Schnitte beruht.

La diseñadora ucraniana afincada en Moscú Erica Zaionts se graduó en la Universidad Estatal del Textil A. N. Kosygin de Moscú. Su firma es una empresa familiar fundada en 2001, y entre sus principales virtudes está la fabricación propia. Erica está considerada una de las diseñadoras de Rusia que crean ropa prêt-à-porter de alta gama. Sus colecciones, mostradas en la Moscow Fashion Week, se caracterizan por su imagen de firmeza y un estilo reconocible, que se basa en la practicidad de las formas.

EWA I WALLA / www.ewaiwalla.se

The Swedish womenswear label Ewa i Walla was established in the early nineties. The designer Ewa Iwalla creates unique garments inspired by the romanticism of the seventeenth century, haute couture and rural culture, and always seeks to achieve an unexpected result. Her collections, distinguished by natural fabrics like cotton, linen, silk or wool, are showcased in the Stockholm Fashion Week and are present in 18 countries through some 320 establishments, including two own stores in Stockholm.

Das schwedische Label für Damenmode wurde Anfang der neunziger Jahre gegründet. Die Designerin Ewa Iwalla kreiert einzigartige Kleidungsstücke, die von der Romantik des 17. Jahrhunderts, Haute-Couture und ländlicher Kultur inspiriert sind und schafft damit stets unerwartete Entwürfe. Ihre Kollektionen zeichnen sich durch natürliche Stoffe wie Baumwolle, Leinen, Seide oder Wolle aus und werden bei der Stockholm Fashion Week gezeigt. Die Mode von Ewa i Walla ist in 18 Ländern in über 320 Geschäften erhältlich, darunter auch die zwei Markenläden in Stockholm.

La firma sueca de moda femenina Ewa i Walla se fundó a principios de los años noventa. Su diseñadora, Ewa Iwalla, crea prendas únicas inspiradas en el romanticismo del siglo xvii, la alta costura y la cultura rural, así que siempre consigue un resultado inesperado. Sus colecciones, que destacan por tejidos naturales como el algodón, el lino, la seda o la lana, se exhiben en la Stockholm Fashion Week y están presentes en 18 países a través de unos 320 establecimientos, entre los que se cuentan las dos tiendas propias en Estocolmo.

G.V.G.V. / www.gvgv.jp

Mug, the Japanese designer behind G.V.G.V., graduated from the Kuwasawa Design School. The label, founded in 1999, stands out for its mix of masculinity and femininity, and conveys great sensitivity each season. G.V.G.V. has become one of the most sought after fashion labels in Tokyo and is a regular during Japan Fashion Week. In addition, Mug is a regular contributor injecting his creativity into other fashion houses.

Mug, die Designerin von G.V.G.V., absolvierte die Kuwasawa Design School. Die 1999 gegründete Marke zeichnet sich durch ihre Mischung aus maskulinen und femininen Einflüssen aus und vermittelt mit jeder Kollektion große Empfindsamkeit. G.V.G.V. hat sich zu einer der attraktivsten Tokioter Modelabels entwickelt und nimmt regelmäßig an der Japan Fashion Week teil. Außerdem arbeitet Mug häufig mit anderen Modefirmen zusammen, die sie mit ihrer Kreativität inspiriert.

Mug, la diseñadora japonesa de G.V.G.V., se graduó en la Escuela de Diseño de Kuwasawa. La firma, fundada en 1999, destaca por su mezcla de masculinidad y feminidad, y trasmite una gran sensibilidad cada temporada. G.V.G.V. se ha convertido en una de las marcas de moda más atractivas de Tokio, y es una habitual del programa oficial de la Japan Fashion Week. Además, Mug es colaboradora asidua de otras firmas de moda a las que inyecta su creatividad.

GEORGIA HARDINGE / www.georgiahardinge.co.uk

Born in London, the daughter of Lord Nick Hardinge and Baroness Florence von Oppenheim grew up traveling and developing her fascination with fashion. She studied at Parsons School in Paris and won the Golden Thimble for her graduation collection. After her return to London, she founded her label in 2009. The launch of her debut collection took place in the independent ONffIOFF runway during London Fashion Week. With the experience of several collections behind her, Georgia has achieved an elegant style marked by architectural touches.

In London als Tochter von Lord Nick Hardinge und der Baronin Florence von Oppenheim geboren, reiste sie bereits in ihrer Kindheit viel und entwickelte eine Faszination mit Design. Sie studierte an der Parsons School in Paris und erhielt für ihre Abschlusskollektion die die Goldmedaille. Nach ihrer Rückkehr nach London gründete sie 2009 ihr Label, dessen offizielle Präsentation im Rahmen der unabhängigen Modenschau ONffIOFF auf der London Fashion Week stattfand. Georgia hat bereits einige Kollektionen herausgebracht und sich einen einzigartigen, eleganten Stil erarbeitet, der sich durch Elemente der Architektur auszeichnet.

Nacida en Londres, hija de lord Nick Hardinge y de la baronesa Florence von Oppenheim, creció viajando y desarrollando su fascinación por el diseño. Estudió en la Escuela Parsons de París y obtuvo el Dedal de Oro por su colección de graduación. Después de su retorno a Londres, creó su firma en 2009, cuya presentación oficial tuvo lugar en la pasarela independiente ONffIOFF durante la London Fashion Week. Con varias colecciones a sus espaldas, Georgia ha conseguido un elegante estilo propio marcado por los toques arquitectónicos.

HARRYHALIM / www.hhharryhalim.com

Born in Indonesia and based in Paris, his first collection won the Asian Young Fashion Designers Contest and he was a finalist in the Mercedes-Benz Asia Fashion Awards in 2005. Later he designed for a commercial fashion house while working on his own collections and perfecting his meticulous technique. In 2008, Harry Halim was awarded Best Young Asian Designer of the Year, which catapulted him to Paris where he shows his modern and romantic collections with a halo of dark sensuality.

Seine erste Kollektion gewann den Asian Young Fashion Designers Contest und 2005 wurde er Finalist bei den Mercedes-Benz Asia Fashion Awards. Später designte er für ein kommerzielles Modehaus und arbeitete nebenher an eigenen Kollektionen, wobei er seine präzise Technik perfektionierte. Im Jahr 2008 wurde er zum besten asiatischen Nachwuchsdesigner des Jahres gewählt. So kam er nach Paris, wo er seitdem seine modernen, romantischen und düstersinnlichen Kollektionen zeigt.

Nacido en Indonesia y afincado en París, su primera colección ganó el Asian Young Fashion Designers Contest y resultó finalista en los Mercedes-Benz Asia Fashion Awards en 2005. Más tarde diseñó para una casa de moda comercial, mientras trabajaba en sus propias colecciones y perfeccionaba su meticulosa técnica. En 2008 fue galardonado como mejor joven diseñador asiático del año, lo que le catapultó a París, donde desde entonces muestra sus colecciones modernas, románticas y con un halo de oscura sensualidad.

HASAN HEJAZI / www.hasanhejazi.co.uk

Hasan Hejazi was born in Manchester. He studied Fine Arts for three years and then decided to move into Fashion Design at Manchester Metropolitan University. He recently completed a Masters in Fashion Design from London College of Fashion. His graduation collection was a success: he was a finalist in Manchester Awards for the best designer fashion and showcased his collection at Harrods Launches. His second collection has an army of followers including celebrities such as Kylie Minogue.

Hasan Hejazi wurde in Manchester geboren. Er studierte drei Jahre Bildende Kunst und entschloss sich dann zu einem Studium des Modedesigns an der Manchester Metropolitan University. Kürzlich schloss er seine Ausbildung mit einem Master in Modedesign des London College of Fashion ab. Seine Abschlusskollektion war ein Erfolg: Er wurde Finalist der Made in Manchester Awards für das beste Modedesign und er stellte seine Kollektion bei den Harrods Launches aus. Seine zweite Kollektion hat bereits eine begeisterte Fangemeinde, darunter Kylie Minogue.

Hasan Hejazi nació en Manchester. Estudió Bellas Artes durante tres años y después decidió cursar Diseño de Moda en la Manchester Metropolitan University. Recientemente ha finalizado el máster en Diseño de Moda del London College of Fashion. Su colección de graduación fue todo un éxito: le llevó a ser finalista en los Premios Manchester al mejor diseñador de moda y se exhibió en Harrods Launches. Su segunda colección cuenta con seguidoras de la relevancia de Kylie Minogue.

IDA SJÖSTEDT / www.idasjostedt.com

Ida Sjöstedt was born in Stockholm. She moved to London and graduated in Fashion Design at Westminster University. In 2001, Ida returned to Sweden and in August of that year she launched her first collection during Stockholm Fashion Week. She has become a regular on this runway since then and she also exhibits in Paris during the prêt-à-porter fashion weeks. The combination of tasteful kitsch and elegance describe Ida's design philosophy. Her aim is to create beautiful clothes for women who want fashion to be fun.

Ida Sjöstedt wurde in Stockholm geboren. Sie zog nach London und absolvierte ein Modedesignstudium an der Westminster University. Im Jahr 2001 ging Ida zurück nach Schweden und im August jenes Jahres stellte sie bei der Modewoche in Stockholm ihre erste Kollektion vor. Seitdem sind ihre Entwürfe dort und auch bei den Prêt-à-Porter-Wochen in Paris regelmäßig zu sehen. Summe aus einer Prise Kitsch vereint mit gutem Geschmack und Eleganz – das ist die Philosophie ihres Designs, das von Frauen bevorzugt wird, für die Mode etwas Spaßiges ist.

Ida Sjöstedt nació en Estocolmo. Se trasladó a Londres y se graduó en Diseño de Moda en la Westminster University. En 2001, Ida regresó a Suecia y en agosto de ese año lanzó su primera colección durante la semana de la moda de Estocolmo, donde desfila desde entonces, y durante las semanas del prêt-à-porter de París. La suma de un toque kitsch con el buen gusto y la elegancia son las claves de su filosofía de diseño, que viste a mujeres para las que la moda es algo divertido.

ION FIZ / www.ionfiz.com

Ion Fiz was born in Bilbao, Spain. He studied at the International School of Fashion Design and Moda Lanca in his native city and has worked for companies such as Karhu, Bonaventure, Elisa Amann and the renowned Pertegaz. After launching his own label, his career has been unstoppable, and has won awards such as the FAD Award for Best Designer, the Prix de la Moda Marie Claire and the L'Oréal Paris Cibeles prize. His proposals have a unique and sophisticated hallmark, which he shows season after season at the Cibeles Madrid Fashion Week.

Ion Fiz wurde in Bilbao (Spanien) geboren. Er studierte an der Escuela Internacional de Diseño y Moda Lanca seiner Heimatstadt und arbeitete für Labels wie Karhu, Bonaventure, Elisa Amann und den Designer Manuel Pertegaz. Die Gründung seines eigenen Unternehmens war überaus erfolgreich und er wurde als Bester Designer mit dem Premio FAD, dem Prix de la Moda Marie Claire dem L'Oréal Paris Cibeles ausgezeichnet. Seine exklusiven und raffinierten Entwürfe zeigt er regelmäßig bei der El Ego de Cibeles Madrid Fashion Week.

Ion Fiz nació en Bilbao (España). Estudió en la Escuela Internacional de Diseño y Moda Lanca de su ciudad y trabajó para firmas como Karhu, Bonaventure, Elisa Amann y el maestro Pertegaz. Tras lanzar su propia firma, su trayectoria ha sido impecable, y se ha ganado reconocimientos como el Premio FAD al Mejor Diseñador, el Prix de la Moda Marie Claire y el L'Oréal París Cibeles. Sus propuestas tienen un sello exclusivo y sofisticado, como demuestra cada temporada en la Cibeles Madrid Fashion Week.

J JS LEE / www.jsleelondon.com

Jackie JS Lee, born in Seoul, Korea, moved to London to study a postgraduate in pattern design at Central Saint Martins. After two years as a pattern designer for Kisa London, she returned to the same school to study an MA. Her graduate collection received rave reviews from the press and buyers, and she was awarded the revered Harrods Award. Later she launched her label J JS Lee, featuring sleek and chic androgynous pieces designed for modern feminine women.

Jackie JS Lee wurde in Seoul (Korea) geboren und zog als Stipendiat nach London, um am Central Saint Martins ein Postgraduiertenstudium in Stoffdesign zu absolvieren. Nach zwei Jahren als Stoffdesigner bei Kisa London kehrte er für ein Masterstudium zu seinem College zurück. Seine Abschlusskollektion wurde von Presse und Einkäufern gelobt mit dem Harrods-Preis ausgezeichnet. Später gründete er sein Label J JS Lee mit androgynen und eleganten Entwürfen für moderne, feminine Frauen.

Jackie JS Lee, nacida en Seúl (Corea), se trasladó a Londres para realizar un posgrado de patronaje en el Central Saint Martins. Después de dos años como patronista en Kisa London, regresó a la misma escuela para cursar un máster. Su colección de graduación recibió muy buenas críticas por parte de la prensa y de los compradores, y la hizo merecedora del venerado Premio Harrods. Más tarde lanzó su marca J JS Lee, con piezas andróginas y elegantes pensadas para una mujer moderna y femenina.

JEAN//PHILLIP / www.jeanphillip.dk

Jean//phillip is a fashion label based in Copenhagen founded by Jean-Phillip in 2007. The main objective of the label is menswear, but each collection also includes a few outfits for women. The Jean//phillip label is both modern and minimalist with a slim cut to create a sense of subtle androgyny suitable for both men and women. Classic tailoring, haute couture and attention to detail are the hallmarks of the designer and his work.

Jean//phillip ist ein Label mit Sitz in Kopenhagen, das 2007 von Jean-Phillip gegründet wurde. Das Unternehmen entwirft hauptsächlich Herrenbekleidung, aber jede Kollektion enthält aus einige Damenmodelle. Das Label Jean//phillip ist avantgardistisch und puristisch, mit schmal geschnittenen Entwürfen, die eine Gefühl dezenter Androgynie vermitteln, das ebenso zu Frauen wie zu Männern passt.. Die klassischen Anzüge sind das Werk eines Couturiers und die Liebe zum Detail sind ein Markenzeichen des Designers und seiner Arbeit.

Jean//phillip es una marca de moda con sede en Copenhague fundada por Jean-Phillip en 2007. El objetivo principal de la marca es la ropa masculina, pero cada colección también incluye algunos estilismos para mujer. La firma de Jean//phillip es vanguardista y minimalista, con un corte *slim*, para crear una sensación de sutil androginia apta tanto para hombres como para mujeres. La sastrería clásica, la mano de obra de alta costura y la atención a los detalles son un sello del diseñador y su obra.

JUANJO OLIVA / www.juanjooliva.com

Juanjo Oliva was born in Madrid. He graduated in Fashion Design in Institución Artística de Enseñanza in his native city and took a course in Fashion Illustration at Parsons School of Design in New York. During the nineties he worked for companies such as Isabel Berz, Zara, Helena Rohner, Antonio Pernas, Sybilla and Amaya Arzuaga. In 2000, he opened his store in Madrid and since 2003 he has showcased his collections at Cibeles Madrid Fashion Week. He has received awards such as the Best L'Oréal Collection, which has been awarded twice, or the T de Telva for the Best National Designer.

Juanjo Oliva wurde in Madrid geboren. Er absolviert ein Modedesignstudium am IADE in seiner Heimatstadt und einen Kurs in Modezeichnung an der Parsons School of Design in New York. In den neunziger Jahren arbeitete er für Firmen wie Isabel Berz, Zara, Helena Rohner, Antonio Pernas, Sybilla und Amaya Arzuaga. Im Jahr 2000 eröffnete er sein erstes Geschäft in Madrid und seit 2003 nimmt er an der Mercedes-Benz Fashion Week Madrid teil. Er wurde mit Preisen ausgezeichnet wie der Auszeichnung für die beste Kollektion von L'Oréal, die er zweimal bekam, oder der T de Telva für den besten nationalen Designer.

Juanjo Oliva nació en Madrid. Se graduó en Diseño de Moda en el IADE de su ciudad y realizó un curso de Ilustración de Moda en la Parsons School of Design de Nueva York. Durante los noventa trabajó para firmas como Isabel Berz, Zara, Helena Rohner, Antonio Pernas, Sybilla y Amaya Arzuaga. En el año 2000 abrió su tienda en Madrid y desde 2003 desfila en la Cibeles Madrid Fashion Week. Atesora premios como el de Mejor Colección de L'Oréal, que le han concedido en dos ocasiones, o el T de Telva al Mejor Diseñador Nacional.

JULIUS / www.julius-garden.jp

The Japanese designer Tastsuro Horikawa started his own line in 1996, creating his first fashion company, Nuke. In 2001, Julius was born as an art project that eventually became a large fashion project combined with video art, its first appearance was in 2004 in Tokyo Collection. It has become a cult label, on account of its gothic style, with black as its trademark color, exploring the spiritual and modern side of the designer.

Der Japaner Tastsuro Horikawa begann mit der Kreation seiner ersten Kleidungslinie im Jahr 1996, die zu seinem ersten Modelabel gehörte: Nuke. In 2001 tat er sich für ein Kunstprojekt mit Julius zusammen. Daraus entwickelte sich schließlich ein großes Modeprojekt, das mit Elementen der Videokunst fusioniert und zum ersten Mal 2004 auf der Tokyo Collection zu sehen war. Als Kultlabel beeindruckt es mit seinem Gothic-Einflüssen, mit Schwarz als zentralem Farbton, das Ausdruck der avantgardistischen und geistigen Seite des Designers ist.

El japonés Tastsuro Horikawa inició con su propia línea de diseño en 1996, creando su primera empresa de moda, Nuke. En 2001 arrancó con Julius como un proyecto de arte, que finalmente se convirtió en un amplio proyecto de moda que fusiona con la videocreación, cuya primera presentación fue en 2004, en Tokio Collection. Convertida en firma de culto, destaca por su tendencia gótica, con el negro como color de referencia, que explora el lado vanguardista y espiritual del diseñador.

KARLOTA LASPALAS / www.karlotalaspalas.com

Karlota Laspalas was born in Pamplona, Spain. Since graduating from the Felicidad Duce School of Fashion and Design, her career knows no limits. She has presented her collections on runways such as 080 Barcelona Fashion, where she received the award for best menswear collection, El Ego de Cibeles Madrid Fashion Week, Creamoda in Bilbao, Createurope in Berlin, and Mittelmoda in Gorizia, Italy. Her proposals, with a bohemian-urban style have conquered both the public and press wherever she exhibits.

Die Designerin Karlota Laspalas wurde im spanischen Pamplona geboren. Seit ihrem Abschluss an der Escuela Superior de Diseño y Moda Felicidad Duce hat sich ihre Karriere unaufhaltsam entwickelt. Ihre Kollektionen hat sie bereits auf Modenschauen wie der 080 Barcelona Fashion vorgestellt, wo sie den Preis für die beste Herrenkollektion gewann, bei der El Ego de Cibeles Madrid Fashion Week, Creamoda in Bilbao, Createurope in Berlin oder Mittelmoda in Gorizia (Italien). In ihren Entwürfe vereinen sich Bohème und städtische Eleganz und sind ein Garant für den Erfolg bei Publikum und Presse.

La diseñadora Karlota Laspalas nació en Pamplona (España). Desde que se graduó en la Escuela Superior de Diseño y Moda Felicidad Duce, su carrera está siendo imparable. Ha presentado sus colecciones en pasarelas como 080 Barcelona Fashion, en la que obtuvo el premio a la mejor colección masculina, El Ego de la Cibeles Madrid Fashion Week, Creamoda, en Bilbao, Createurope, en Berlín, o Mittelmoda, en Gorizia (Italia). Sus propuestas, con un carácter entre bohemio y urbano, conquistan a público y prensa allá donde se exhiben.

KRIS VAN ASSCHE / www.krisvanassche.com

Born in Belgium, Kris Van Assche is a graduate of the Royal Academy of Fine Arts in Antwerp, and later joined Hedi Slimane's team at YSL in Paris. When Slimane joined Dior Homme in 2003, Van Assche followed suit. In 2005, he created his own label and in 2007 he was appointed artistic director of Dior Homme, combining both jobs perfectly. Van Assche has a unique approach to sportswear, blending luxurious and functional materials for a modern and sophisticated man.

In Belgien geboren, absolvierte Kris Van Assche die Königliche Akademie der Schönen Künste von Antwerpen und wurde daraufhin Teil des Teams um Hedi Slimane bei YSL in Paris. Als Slimano 2003 zu Dior ging, folgte ihm Van Assche. Im Jahr 2005 gründete er sein eigenes Unternehmen, 2007 wurde er künstlerischer Leiter bei Dior Homme und vereinte seine beiden Tätigkeiten perfekt. Van Assche besitzt ein einzigartiges Talent für Sportmode, bei der er luxuriöse und funktionale Materialien vereint und Entwürfe für den eleganten, weltgewandten Mann kreiert.

Nacido en Bélgica, Kris Van Assche se graduó en la Real Academia de Bellas Artes de Amberes, y se incorporó después al equipo de Hedi Slimane en YSL, en París. Cuando Slimane fichó por Dior Homme en 2003, Van Assche siguió sus pasos. En 2005 creó su propia firma y en 2007 fue nombrado director artístico de Dior Homme, combinando ambos trabajos a la perfección. Van Assche posee un enfoque único para la ropa deportiva, mezclando materiales lujosos y funcionales para un hombre moderno y sofisticado.

LEMONIEZ / www.lemoniez.com

Fernando Lemoniez was born in San Sebastian, Spain, where in 1985 he opened a boutique-atelier with his own collections. He later moved to Paris, and attended a training course at Yves Saint Laurent Haute Couture and presented his collections within the official calendar of the Chambre Syndicale de la Couture. Between 1991 and 1998, he joined forces with Miguel Palacio to create Palacio & Lemoniez, a label which used to showcase its collections at Cibeles Madrid, where he presents his runway shows solo since 1999.

Fernando Lemoniez wurde in San Sebastián (Spanien) geboren, wo er 1985 ein Boutique-Atelier mit eigenen Kollektionen eröffnete. Nach seinem Umzug nach Paris perfektionierte er bei Yves Saint Laurent Haute Couture sein Können und präsentierte seine Kollektionen im Rahmen des offiziellen Programms des Chambre Syndicale de la Couture. Von 1991 bis 1998 arbeitete er mit Miguel Palacio zusammen und schuf Palacio & Lemoniez, das seine Entwürfe bei der Cibeles Madrid vorstellte, wo er seine Entwürfe seit 1999 alleine zeigt.

Fernando Lemoniez nació en San Sebastián (España), donde en 1985 abrió una *boutique-atelier* con colecciones propias. Posteriormente se trasladó París, realizó un curso de perfeccionamiento en Yves Saint Laurent Haute Couture y presentó sus colecciones dentro del calendario oficial de la Chambre Syndicale de la Couture. Entre 1991 y 1998 se alió con Miguel Palacio para la creación de Palacio & Lemoniez, que presentaba sus colecciones en Cibeles Madrid, donde ahora desfila en solitario desde el año 1999.

MAISON MARTIN MARGIELA
www.maisonmartinmargiela.com

The label was founded in 1988 by Martin Margiela, a graduate from the Royal Academy of Fine Arts in Antwerp and creative director of Hermès, and Jenny Meirens, assistant to Jean Paul Gaultier. A must at Paris Fashion Week, and having celebrated its 20th Anniversary, Maison Martin Margiela continues to wow with unique propositions and international repercussions. With Renzo Rosso now at the forefront of the label, a new era of creative identity can be expected without overlooking the essence of the mythical house.

Das Unternehmen wurde 1988 gegründet von Martin Margiela, einem Absolventen der Königlichen Akademie der Schönen Künste von Antwerpen und Kreativdirektor von Hermes, und Jenny Meirens, Assistentin von Jean Paul Gaultier. Mit 20jähriger Erfahrung ist Maison Martin Margiela als Label mit internationalem Ruf eine feste Größe der Paris Fashion Week und überrascht noch immer mit einzigartigen Entwürfen. Der Wechsel von Renzo Rosso in die Unternehmensleitung verspricht eine neue kreative Identität, ohne die Essenz des mythischen Modehauses vergessen zu lassen.

La firma fue creada en 1988 por Martin Margiela, graduado en la Real Academia de las Bellas Artes de Amberes y director creativo de Hermès, y Jenny Meirens, asistente de Jean Paul Gaultier. Indispensable en la Paris Fashion Week y tras haber superado ya su vigesimo aniversario, Maison Martin Margiela sigue sorprendiendo con propuestas únicas y una repercusión internacional. El relevo de Renzo Rosso al mando de la firma promete una nueva identidad creativa sin olvidar la esencia de la mítica casa.

MAL-AIMÉE / www.mal-aimee.com

Léonie Hostettler and Marius Borgeaud met in the ateliers of the Geneva University of Art and Design. They have been working together since their beginnings at Nina Ricci with Olivier Theyskens. In 2010, they presented their first womenswear collection in Paris under the name of Mal-Aimée. They experiment with volumes and lines, paying particular attention to the choice of colors and fabrics. Simultaneously poetic, romantic, sporty and urban, their proposals oscillate between extreme femininity and elegant androgyny.

Die Designer Léonie Hostettler und Marius Borgeaud lernten sich in den Ateliers der Hochschule für Kunst und Gestaltung in Genf kennen und arbeiteten seit ihren Anfängen bei Nina Ricci mit Olivier Theyskens zusammen. Im Jahr 2010 präsentierten in Paris ihre erste Kollektion unter dem Namen Mal-Aimée. Sie experimentieren mit Volumen und Linien und legen besondere Aufmerksamkeit auf die Auswahl von Farben und Stoffen. Ihre Entwürfe sind poetisch, romantisch, sportlich und urban und bewegen sich zwischen extremer Weiblichkeit und Androgynität.

Los diseñadores Léonie Hostettler y Marius Borgeaud se conocieron en los talleres de la Escuela Superior de Arte y Diseño de Ginebra y trabajaron juntos desde sus inicios en Nina Ricci, con Olivier Theyskens. En 2010 presentaron en París su primera colección bajo el nombre de Mal-Aimée. Experimentan con volúmenes y líneas prestando especial atención a la selección de colores y tejidos. Sus propuestas, entre la extrema feminidad y la androginia elegante, son poéticas, románticas, *sport* y urbanas.

MALAFACHA BRAND / malafacha.blogspot.com

The Mexican designers Francisco Saldaña and Víctor Hernal are the duo behind Malafacha Brand, a male and female clothing label. Francisco studied Fashion Design and Victor studied Visual Communication, both disciplines have helped in developing a product with a very personal style. Winners of the prize for best womenswear collection in Mexico Fashion Awards for their fall/winter 2008/2009 collection, they present their collections at Mercedes-Benz Fashion Week Mexico.

Die mexikanischen Designer Francisco Saldaña und Víctor Hernal sind das Duo hinter dem Label für Herren- und Damenkleidung Malafacha Brand. Francisco studierte Modedesign und Víctor absolviert den Studiengang Visuelle Kommunikation. Beide Ausbildungen halfen ihnen bei der Entwicklung ihres sehr eigenwilligen Modestils. Als Gewinner des Preises für die beste Damenkollektion für Herbst/Winter 2008-2009 bei den Mexico Fashion Awards präsentieren sie ihre Entwürfe bei der Mercedes-Benz Fashion Week Mexico.

Los diseñadores mexicanos Francisco Saldaña y Víctor Hernal conforman el dúo que está detrás de la firma de ropa masculina y femenina Malafacha Brand. El primero estudió Diseño de Moda, y el segundo, Comunicación Visual: ambas disciplinas les han ayudado en el desarrollo de un producto con un estilo muy personal. Ganadores del premio a la mejor colección femenina en los Mexico Fashion Awards por su colección otoño-invierno 2008-2009, presentan sus colecciones en la Mercedes-Benz Fashion Week Mexico.

MALINI RAMANI / www.maliniramani.com

Born in New York, she spent a few years in India and then returned to her hometown to study Fashion Buying and Merchandising at the Fashion Institute of Technology. Then she decided to create her own label in India. Her philosophy is to design clothes that she would wear herself. She believes glamorous, vibrant colors and plunging necklines. She has her own stores in India and Bali, and her collections are sold in cities around the world, including Hong Kong, Monte Carlo and New York.

In New York geboren, verbrachte sie einige Jahre in Indien und ging später in ihre Geburtsstadt zurück, um am Fashion Institute of Technology Fashion Buying und Merchandising zu studieren. Dann beschloss sie, in Indien ihr eigenes Label zu gründen. Ihre Philosophie besteht darin, Kleidung zu entwerfen, die sie selbst tragen kann. Dabei setzt sie auf glamouröse, lebhafte Farben und raffinierte Ausschnitte. Sie hat eigene Filialen in Indien und Bali, und ihre Kollektionen werden in Städten weltweit verkauft, darunter Hongkong, Monte Carlo und New York.

Nacida en Nueva York, pasó algunos años en la India y luego regresó a su ciudad natal para estudiar Fashion Buying and Merchandising en el Fashion Institute of Technology. Después decidió crear su propia firma, en la India. Su filosofía es diseñar prendas que ella misma pueda vestir, mientras apuesta por colores glamorosos y vibrantes y escotes pronunciados. Cuenta con tiendas propias en la India y en Bali, y sus colecciones se venden en ciudades de todo el mundo, como Hong Kong, Montecarlo o Nueva York.

MANISH ARORA / www.manisharora.ws

Arora is considered as the John Galliano of India. He studied at the National Institute of Fashion Technology and founded his firm in 1997. In 2002, he opened his first store in New Delhi and the following year another one in Bombay. His success and international prestige, and his regular presence in the fashion weeks in India and London, led him to open new stores and to sell in more than eighty stores worldwide. His blend of Indian tradition with western silhouettes and eccentric colors are the trademarks of the label.

Arora gilt als der John Galliano Indiens. Er studierte am National Institute of Fashion Technology und gründete sein Label im Jahr 1997. In 2002 eröffnete er sein erstes Geschäft in Neu-Delhi und im darauf folgenden Jahr ein weiteres in Bombay. Durch seinen internationalen Ruf und Erfolg sowie seine regelmäßige Präsenz bei den Modewochen in Indien und London eröffnete er weitere Standorte und er verkauft seine Entwürfe in mehr als 80 Geschäften weltweit. Seine Fusion aus indischer Tradition mit westlicher Schnittführung und extravaganten Farben sind das Markenzeichen des Labels.

Arora está considerado el John Galliano de la India. Estudió en el National Institute of Fashion Technology y creó su firma en 1997. En 2002 abrió su primera tienda en Nueva Delhi y al año siguiente otra en Bombay. Su éxito y prestigio internacional, así como su presencia habitual en las semanas de la moda de la India y de Londres, le lleva a abrir nuevos establecimientos y a vender en más de ochenta tiendas de todo el mundo. Su mezcla de tradición india con siluetas occidentales y colores excéntricos son el símbolo de la firma.

MARCEL OSTERTAG / www.marcelostertag.com

Marcel Ostertag was born in Berchtesgaden, Germany. After completing his studies in ESMOD Munich, he graduated from Central Saint Martins. Then, he decided to create his own label, whose spectacular debut in 2006 was praised by the press and recognized with awards such as Moët & Chandon Fashion Debut and the Karstadt New Generation Award. Today, he has his own store in Munich and his collections are presented during the official calendar of the Mercedes-Benz Fashion Week Berlin.

Marcel Ostertag wurde in Berchtesgaden geboren. Er begann sein Modestudium an der ESMOD München und machte seinen Abschluss am Central Saint Martins. Nach seiner Ausbildung gründete er sein eigenes Label, dessen spektakuläres Debüt 2006 von der Presse gefeiert und mit Auszeichnungen wie dem Moët & Chandon Fashion Debut oder dem Karstadt New Generation Award bedacht wurde. Heute hat er ein eigenes Atelier in München und seine Kollektionen werden beim offiziellen Programm der Mercedes-Benz Fashion Week Berlin präsentiert.

Marcel Ostertag nació en Berchtesgaden (Alemania). Después de cursar sus estudios en ESMOD Múnich, se graduó en el Central Saint Martins. Tras finalizar su formación decide crear su firma, cuyo espectacular debut en 2006 fue alabado por la prensa y reconocido con premios como el Moët & Chandon Fashion Debut o el Karstadt New Generation Award. Hoy tiene tienda propia en Múnich y sus colecciones están presentes en el programa oficial de la Mercedes-Benz Fashion Week Berlin.

MARK FAST / www.markfast.net

The Canadian knitwear designer Mark Fast studied for five years at Central Saint Martins in London. He has created knitwear for Bora Aksu, a collaboration that spanned three seasons, and has worked as well with Stuart Vevers for the Loewe fall/winter 2009 show and with Christian Louboutin on shoes for his spring/summer 2010 collection. His collections, which combines different techniques and innovative materials, are exhibited at London Fashion Week and featured in magazines such as *Vogue, i-D* and *Another Magazine*.

Der kanadische Designer für Strickwaren Mark Fast studierte fünf Jahre am Central Saint Martins in London. Drei Saisons arbeitete er mit Bora Aksu am Design für Strickwaren für dessen Kollektionen zusammen, er unterstützte Stuart Vevers bei seiner Loewe-Kollektion Herbst/Winter 2009 und war an der Schuhkollektion von Christian Louboutin für Frühjahr/Sommer 2010 beteiligt. Seine Kollektionen, in denen er unterschiedliche Stricktechniken und innovative Materialien kombiniert, waren bei der London Fashion Week und in Zeitschriften wie *Vogue, i-D* oder *Another Magazine* zu sehen.

El diseñador de punto canadiense Mark Fast estudió durante cinco años en el Central Saint Martins de Londres. Ha colaborado durante tres temporadas con Bora Aksu en el diseño de punto para sus colecciones, para Stuart Vevers en la colección de Loewe otoño-invierno 2009 y en la de calzado de Christian Louboutin primavera-verano 2010. Sus colecciones, en las que combina diferentes técnicas de punto y materiales innovadores, se exhiben en la London Fashion Week y aparecen en revistas como *Vogue, i-D* o *Another Magazine*.

MARTA MONTOTO / www.martamontoto.com

The young Spanish designer Marta Montoto, born in Galicia, comes from a family background in textile. Her family has worked in knitwear since the fifties, so she dares to experiment and redefine concepts using this technique that she dominates so well. She studied Fashion Design at ESDEGMA. After completing work experience in Armand Basi, she has decided to design highly creative collections for men, with naïve touches, which have earned her a place on runways such as El Ego de Cibeles Madrid Fashion Week.

Die junge spanische Designerin Marta Montoto wurde in Galicien geboren und stammt aus einer Familie von Textilfachleuten, die seit den 50er Jahren Strickwaren herstellt. Daher wagte sie eine experimentelle Herangehensweise und definierte Konzepte durch ihre Technik neu, die sie meisterhaft beherrscht. Sie studierte Modedesign an der ESDEGMA. Nach ihrem Abschluss und Praktika bei Armand Basi begann sie mit dem Entwurf sehr kreativer Herrenkollektionen mit naiven Anklängen, die ihr bei Modenschauen wie der El Ego de Cibeles Madrid Fashion Week große Anerkennung einbrachten.

La joven diseñadora española Marta Montoto, nacida en Galicia, viene de tradición textil, puesto que su familia trabajaba el punto desde los años cincuenta, por lo que se atreve a experimentar y redefinir conceptos mediante esta técnica que tanto domina. Estudió Diseño de Moda en ESDEGMA. Tras finalizar y realizar prácticas en Armand Basi, ha apostado por diseñar colecciones para hombre muy creativas, con toques naïfs, que le han valido un hueco en pasarelas como El Ego de Cibeles Madrid Fashion Week.

MARTIN LAMOTHE / www.martinlamothe.es

Elena Martin was born in Barcelona. She graduated from the Escola d'Arts i Tècniques de la Moda in her native city, and later studied Art History and earned an honors degree at the Southampton Art School. She then moved to London and studied at Central Saint Martins. After graduation, Elena worked with Alexander McQueen, Vivienne Westwood and Robert Cary-Williams. In 2006, she launched her label Martin Lamothe, with an impeccable career and appearances on runways in Berlin, Barcelona, Paris or Madrid.

Elena Martín wurde in Barcelona geboren. Sie absolvierte die Escuela de Artes y Técnicas de Moda in ihrer Heimatstadt, studierte später Kunstgeschichte und schloss die Southampton Art School mit Auszeichnung ab. Nach ihrem Umzug nach London studierte sie am Central Saint Martins. Nach ihrem Abschluss arbeitete Elena für Alexander McQueen, Vivienne Westwood und Robert Cary-Williams. Im Jahr 2006 gründete sie ihr Label Martin Lamothe, das sofort ein Erfolg wurde und dessen Entwürfe bereits bei Modenschauen in Berlin, Barcelona, Paris oder Madrid zu sehen waren.

Elena Martín nació en Barcelona. Se graduó en la Escuela de Artes y Técnicas de Moda de su ciudad y más tarde estudió Historia del Arte y obtuvo matrícula de honor en la Southampton Art School. Luego se trasladó a Londres y estudió en el Central Saint Martins. Tras graduarse, Elena trabajó con Alexander McQueen, Vivienne Westwood y Robert Cary-Williams. En 2006 lanzó su firma Martin Lamothe, con una trayectoria impecable y apariciones en pasarelas de Berlín, Barcelona, París o Madrid.

MAYA HANSEN / www.mayahansen.com

Maya Hansen was born in Madrid. She graduated with honors at the CSDMM in Madrid in 2002, after having already received some recognition. After her experience in Javier Larraínzar's atelier, she founded her label in 2004 and since 2006, she has specialized in corsetry. She has presented her proposals in fairs such as Erotica UK, which brings together the world's best corset makers, and has earned a spot in the Cibeles Madrid Fashion Week calendar.

Maya Hansen wurde in Madrid geboren. Sie schloss ihr Studium des Modedesign am Centro Superior de Diseño de Moda in Madrid im Jahr 2002 mit Auszeichnung ab, nachdem sie bereits einige Anerkennung erhalten hatte. Nach ihrer Tätigkeit im Atelier von Javier Larraínzar, gründete sie 2004 ihr Label und seit 2006 spezialisiert sie sich in der Fertigung von Korsetts. Sie stellte ihre Entwürfe bei Messen wie der Erotica UK vor, wo die besten Korsetts der Welt zu sehen sind, und konnte sich mit ihren Entwürfen eine wohl verdiente Nische im Programm der Cibeles Madrid Fashion Week erobern.

Maya Hansen nació en Madrid. Se graduó con matrícula de honor en el Centro Superior de Diseño de Moda de Madrid en 2002, tras haber recibido ya algunos reconocimientos. Después de su experiencia en el taller de Javier Larraínzar, fundó su firma en 2004 y desde 2006 se especializa en corsetería. Ha presentado sus propuestas en ferias como Erotica UK, donde se dan cita los mejores corseteros del mundo, y se ha ganado un merecido hueco en la agenda de la Cibeles Madrid Fashion Week.

NEREA LURGAIN / www.nerealurgain.com

Nerea Lurgain was born in San Sebastian, Spain. She graduated in Fine Arts in Lejona and Fashion Design in IDEP Barcelona. Nerea works in different areas of design and art, which gives her ideas, sources of inspiration and design mechanisms that differentiates her with a unique and personal way to project items. She has presented her collection at 080 Barcelona Fashion Week, the Dalian International Show in China, the Cibeles Madrid Fashion Week and the China International Garment & Textile Fair.

Nerea Lurgain wurde im spanischen San Sebastián geboren. Sie absolvierte ein Kunststudium in Lejona und studierte Modedesign am IDEP in Barcelona. Nerea ist in verschiedenen Design- und Kunstbereichen tätig. Daraus speist sich ihr Ideenreichtum, ihre Tätigkeit wirkt als Inspirationsquelle und sie immer lernt neue Designtechniken kennen, die ihr einen einzigartigen und persönlichen Stil verleihen. Ihre Entwürfe waren bereits auf der 080 Barcelona Fashion Week, bei der Dalian International Show in China, der Cibeles Madrid Fashion Week und auf der Messe China Internacional Garment & Textile zu sehen.

Nerea Lurgain nació en San Sebastián. Se graduó en Bellas Artes en Lejona y en Diseño de Moda en el IDEP de Barcelona. Nerea se desenvuelve en diferentes áreas del diseño y del arte, lo que le confiere ideas, fuentes de inspiración y mecanismos de diseño que le otorgan una manera única y personal de proyectar prendas. Ha presentado sus propuestas en la 080 Barcelona Fashion Week, en el Dalian International Show en China, en la Cibeles Madrid Fashion Week y en la feria China International Garment & Textile.

OMAR KASHOURA / www.omarkashoura.com

Born in Leeds, United Kingdom, of Arab descent, Omar Kashoura graduated with honors from the London College of Fashion with a collection that won him the award for best menswear designer in New York's Gen Art Style. He worked for labels such as Preen and Unconditional, and in 2006 he completed his Masters at Central Saint Martins. Since the launch of his successful label, he has received awards such as the Deutsche Bank Pyramid Award and the NewGen from the British Fashion Council for two consecutive seasons.

In Leeds im Vereinigten Königreich geboren und arabischer Herkunft, absolvierte Omar Kashoura sein Studium mit Auszeichnung am London College of Fashion. Er zeigte eine Abschlusskollektion, mit der er den Preis für den besten Designer für Herrenmode bei den New York Gen Art Style. Er arbeitete für Marken wie Preen und Unconditional und 2006 machte er seinen Master am Central Saint Martins. Seit der Gründung seines erfolgreichen Labels erhielt er Auszeichnungen wie den Deutsche Bank Pyramid Award und an zwei aufeinander folgenden Saisons den NewGen des British Fashion Council.

Nacido en Leeds (Reino Unido) y de ascendencia árabe, Omar Kashoura se graduó con honores en el London College of Fashion, con una colección que le valió el premio al mejor diseñador de moda masculina en los premios New York's Gen Art Style. Trabajó para firmas como Preen y Unconditional, y en 2006 finalizó su máster en el Central Saint Martins. Desde el lanzamiento de su exitosa firma, ha recibido premios como el Deutsche Bank Pyramid Award y el NewGen del Consejo Británico de la Moda en dos temporadas seguidas.

QASIMI / www.qasimi.com

From the United Arab Emirates, Khalid Al Qasimi grew up influenced by the sophistication of the Middle East. In 2001, he graduated in Hispanic Studies and French Literature at University College London, and later decided to study Fashion Design at Central Saint Martins. From 2008, he has presented several womenswear and menswear collections in the London Fashion Week, and since 2009 he is on the calendar of the Paris Men's Fashion Week. Currently he concentrates on men's fashion.

Khalid Al Qasimi stammt aus den Vereinigten Arabischen Emiraten und ist sehr vom eleganten Stil des Nahen Ostens geprägt. Im Jahr 2001 machte er seinen Abschluss in Spanisch und französischer Literatur am University College London und später entschied er sich zu einem Studium des Modedesigns am Central Saint Martins. Seit 2008 stellte er bei der London Fashion Week verschiedene Kollektionen für Damen und Herren vor, und seit 2009 ist er auch auf der Paris Men's Fashion Week vertreten. Aktuell konzentriert er sich auf Herrenmode.

Procedente de los Emiratos Árabes, Khalid Al Qasimi creció influenciado por la sofisticación de Oriente Medio. En 2001 se graduó en Estudios Hispánicos y Literatura Francesa en el University College London, y más tarde decidió estudiar Diseño de Moda en el Central Saint Martins. Desde 2008 ha presentado varias colecciones de mujer y hombre en la London Fashion Week, y desde 2009 está presente en la agenda de la Paris Men's Fashion Week. Actualmente se centra en la moda masculina.

RICARDO DOURADO / www.ricardodourado.com

Ricardo Dourado was born in Portugal. He completed his studies in 2003 at CITEX Oporto. He has worked in studios such as Osvaldo Martins, Lidija Kolovrat and Helena de Matos. In 2004, Ricardo established his own atelier, and has since presented his collections at ModaLisboa Fashion Week. He is also a member of the design team Polopique, a fashion company based in Portugal, Brazil and Spain. His work conveys a casual elegance and challenges conventional forms.

Ricardo Dourado wurde in Portugal geboren. Im Jahr 2003 beendete er seine Studien an der Fachhochschule für Textil in Porto. Er arbeitete für Label wie Osvaldo Martins, Lidija Kolovrat oder Helena de Matos. In 2004 eröffnete er sein eigenes Atelier und seitdem präsentiert er seine Kollektionen bei der ModaLisboa Fashion Week. Er gehört außerdem zum Designteam Polopique, einem Modeunternehmen mit Standorten in Portugal, Brasilien und Spanien. Seine Entwürfe vermitteln mühelose Eleganz und stellen konventionelle Formen in Frage.

Ricardo Dourado nació en Portugal. Finalizó sus estudios en 2003 en el Centro de Formación Profesional de la Industria Textil de Oporto. Ha trabajado en estudios como los de Osvaldo Martins, Lidija Kolovrat o Helena de Matos. En 2004 crea su propio *atelier*, y desde entonces presenta sus colecciones en ModaLisboa Fashion Week y forma parte del equipo de diseño de Polopique, una empresa de moda con sedes en Portugal, Brasil y España. Sus trabajo transmite una elegancia desenfadada y cuestiona las formas convencionales.

SINPATRON / www.sinpatron.com

As the name suggests, the Spanish company created by Alberto Etxebarrieta from Bilbao is characterized by modeling his garments, because it gives him greater freedom than patternmaking does. He studied Tourism in his hometown and Dramatic Art in Edinburgh, until his life "without patterns" led him to fashion. He is self-taught and a craftsman. He created the label Sinpatron in 2004 and presents his collections at the Cibeles Madrid Fashion Week with bold, colorful unisex proposals.

Die Mode des aus Bilbao in Spanien stammenden Alberto Etxebarrieta zeichnet sich durch die innovativen Formen seiner Entwürfe aus, die für mehr Bewegungsfreiheit sorgen als figurnahe Schnitte. In seiner Heimatstadt studierte er Tourismus und in Edinburgh Theater, bis er die Mode entdeckte, wo er als Autodidakt und Handwerker erfolgreich ist. Im Jahr 2004 gründete er die Marke Sinpatron und präsentiert seine mutigen, bunten Unisex-Entwürfe auf der Cibeles Madrid Fashion Week.

Como su nombre indica, la firma española creada por el bilbaíno Alberto Etxebarrieta se caracteriza por el modelaje de sus prendas, que le proporciona mayor libertad que los patrones. Estudió Turismo en su ciudad natal y Arte Dramático en Edimburgo, hasta que su vida «sin patrón» le llevó a la moda, de la que es autodidacta y artesano. Creó la marca Sinpatron en 2004 y presenta sus colecciones en la Cibeles Madrid Fashion Week, con atrevidas y coloristas propuestas unisex.

SPIJKERS EN SPIJKERS / www.spijkersenspijkers.nl

The Dutch twin sisters Truus and Riet created the label Spijkers en Spijkers in 2000, after graduating from the School of Arts in Arnhem. For their debut collection, they were awarded the Robijn Fashion Award, and they completed a Masters at the Fashion Institute in the same city. Inspired by their idols, Schiaparelli and Vionnet, they use their individuality with a common vision, thus achieving solid, clear and geometric forms highlighting the female figure. They have presented their collections in London, Amsterdam and Milan.

Die holländischen Zwillinge Truus und Riet gründeten das Label Spijkers en Spijkers im Jahr 2000, nachdem sie an der Kunsthochschule Arnhem studiert hatten. Inspiriert von ihren Idolen Schiaparelli und Vionnet, nutzen sie ihre Individualität mit gemeinsamer Vision und schaffen solide, klare und geometrische Formen, die die weibliche Figur zur Geltung bringen. Ihre Kollektionen zeigten sie bereits in London, Amsterdam und Mailand.

Las gemelas holandesas Truus y Riet crearon la firma Spijkers en Spijkers en el año 2000, tras graduarse en la Escuela de Artes de Arnhem (obteniendo por su debut el Premio Robijn de la Moda) y realizar un máster en el Instituto de la Moda de la misma ciudad. Inspiradas en sus ídolos, Schiaparelli y Vionnet, utilizan su individualidad con una visión común, consiguiendo así formas sólidas, claras y geométricas que resaltan la figura femenina. Han desfilado en Londres, Ámsterdam y Milán.

STAS LOPATKIN / www.lopatkin.ru

Stas Lopatkin was born in Leningrad. He studied at the School of Sewing and Graphic Arts Department of the Herzen State Pedagogical University of Russia. After graduating, he began with theatrical costume design and for private orders, until he created his own label in 2001. He made his debut in 2003 at the Saint Petersburg Fashion Week, and has since showcased his collections for the Russian and European public with proposals that always combine elegance and fine art as a hallmark.

Stas Lopatkin wurde in Sankt Petersburg geboren. Er studierte an der Schule für Schneiderkunst und der Fakultät für Grafische Kunst der Staatlichen Pädagogische Herzen-Universität in Russland. Nach seinem Abschluss begann er, Theaterkostüme und Modelle für Privatkunden zu entwerfen, bis er 2001 sein eigenes Unternehmen gründete. Er debütierte 2003 auf der Saint Petersburg Fashion Week und präsentiert seine Kollektionen seither dem russischen und europäischen Publikum. Er begeistert mit Entwürfen, bei denen er praktische Eleganz mit feinster Schneiderkunst zur Harmonie verhilft – das ist sein Markenzeichen.

Stas Lopatkin nació en Leningrado. Estudió en la Escuela de Costura y en el Departamento de Artes Gráficas de la Universidad Pedagógica Estatal Herzen de Rusia. Tras graduarse, comenzó con el diseño de vestuario teatral y para particulares, hasta que en 2001 creó su propia firma. Debutó en 2003 en la Saint Petersburg Fashion Week, y desde entonces presenta sus colecciones para el público ruso y europeo, con unas propuestas que siempre armonizan la elegancia práctica y el arte refinado como sello de identidad.

HÖGSKOLAN I BORÅS
VETENSKAP FÖR PROFESSION

THE SWEDISH SCHOOL OF TEXTILES / www.hb.se

Sara Andersson, Johanna Milvert, Elin Klevmar, Stina Randestad, Emelie Johansson, Jennie Siljedahl, Elin Sundling, Ellinor Nilsen, Charlotta Mattsson, David Söderlund, Helena Quist.

In the Swedish School of Textiles of the University of Borås, fashion design is understood in its broadest sense. The school provides a unique environment for reaching maturity as a designer and artist. This book features the collections created by designers who passed through its classrooms in recent years and who presented their collections in the spring/summer 2011 edition of Stockholm Fashion Week. The proposals are a sign of creativity and the immense talent of these young designers.

An der Swedish School of Textiles der Universiät Borås, werden zahlreiche Aspekte des Modedesigns gelehrt. Die Schule bietet ein einzigartiges Umfeld zum Erreichen des Abschlusses als Designer und Künstler. In diesem Buch stellen wir die verschiedenen Kollektionen von Designern vor, die in den letzten Jahren diese Schule absolvierten und ihre Entwürfe im Frühjahr/Sommer 2011 im Rahmen der Stockholm Fashion Week präsentierten. Die Entwürfe zeigen die Kreativität und das große Talent dieser jungen Designer.

En la Swedish School of Textiles de la Universidad de Borås, el diseño de moda se entiende en su sentido más amplio. La escuela proporciona un entorno único para alcanzar la madurez como diseñador y artista. En este libro presentamos las diferentes colecciones ideadas por los diseñadores formados en sus aulas en los últimos años, que se presentaron en la edición primavera-verano 2011 de la Stockholm Fashion Week..

TIM VAN STEENBERGEN / www.timvansteenbergen.com

The Belgian designer Tim Van Steenbergen graduated from the Royal Academy of Fine Arts in Antwerp. Afterwards he studied draping and haute couture and worked as chief assistant for Olivier Theyskens. In 2002, he presented his first collection in Paris and created his own label. In addition to his magnificent collections, Tim creates costumes for major movie and theater productions worldwide. In 2009 he was voted best Belgian designer in the Elle Style Awards.

Der belgische Designer Tim Van Steenbergen ist Absolvent der Königlichen Akademie der Schönen Künste von Antwerpen. Daraufhin wurde er in Schneiderkunst und Haute-Couture ausgebildet und arbeitete als Hauptassistent für Olivier Theyskens. Im Jahr 2002 präsentierte in Paris seine erste Kollektion und gründete sein eigenes Label. Neben seinen wunderbaren Kollektionen entwirft Tim Kostüme für wichtige Kino- und Theaterproduktionen in aller Welt. Im Jahr 2009 wurde er bei den Elle Style Awards zum besten belgischen Designer ausgezeichnet.

El diseñador belga Tim Van Steenbergen se graduó en la Real Academia de Bellas Artes de Amberes. Después recibió clases de drapeado y alta costura y trabajó como asistente principal de Olivier Theyskens. En 2002 presentó su primera colección en París y creó su propia firma. Además de sus magníficas colecciones, Tim crea vestuario para importantísimas producciones de cine y teatro de todo el mundo. En 2009 fue elegido mejor diseñador belga en los Elle Style Awards.

TSUMORI CHISATO / www.tsumorichisato.com

Born in Japan, Tsumori Chisato studied at the prestigious Bunka Fashion College in Tokyo. Later she worked as head designer for the Issey Miyake Sports line, later renamed I. S. Chisato Tsumori Design. In 1990, she presented her own collection Tsumori Chisato and at Japan Fashion Week, where it was a total success. In 2003, she presented her menswear collection and became part of the official calendar of the Paris Fashion Week with innovation, elegance and fun as hallmarks.

In Japan geboren, studierte Tsumori Chisato an der prestigeträchtigsten Modeschule Bunka in Tokio. Später arbeitete sie als Chefdesignerin von Issey Miyake an seiner Linie Issey Sports, die später in I. S. Chisato Tsumori Design umbenannt wurde. In 1990 präsentierte sie ihre eigene Kollektion unter dem Namen Tsumori Chisato auf der Japan Fashion Week, wo er einen großen Erfolg feierte. Im Jahr 2003 zeigte sie ihre Herrenkollektion und wurde mit seinem innovativen, eleganten und amüsanten Stil Teil des offiziellen Programms der Paris Fashion Week.

Nacida en Japón, Tsumori Chisato estudió en la prestigiosa Escuela de Moda Bunka de Tokio. Más tarde comenzó a trabajar como diseñadora principal de Issey Miyake en su línea Issey Sports, después renombrada I. S. Chisato Tsumori Design. En 1990 presentó colección propia como Tsumori Chisato en la Japan Fashion Week, donde cosechó un gran éxito. En 2003 presentó una colección masculina y entró a formar parte del programa oficial de la Paris Fashion Week con un sello innovador, elegante y divertido.

VASSILIOS KOSTETSOS / www.kostetsos.gr

Vassilios Kostetsos was born in Athens, where his mother had a leading fashion import business. By the age of nine, he visited the studio and was enchanted with this magical world. In 1990, he created his own label and presented his first haute couture collection with excellent results. He has presented runway shows in places as special as the Central Railway Station of Athens, and his collections have received critical claim from followers in New York.

Vassilios Kostetsos wurde in Athen geboren, wo seine Mutter ein bekanntes Importgeschäft für Mode führte. Mit neun Jahren besuchte er ihr Studio und war von da an von dieser magischen Welt gefesselt. Im Jahr 1990 gründete er sein eigenes Unternehmen und präsentierte seine erste Haute-Couture-Kollektion mit hervorragenden Ergebnissen. Er organisierte Modenschauen an besonderen Orten wie dem Hauptbahnhof von Athen und seine letzten Kollektionen wurden vom New Yorker Publikum hoch gelobt.

Vassilios Kostetsos nació en Atenas, donde su madre tenía un reconocido negocio de importación de moda. A los nueve años visitó su estudio, y entonces quedó impregnado de ese mágico mundo. En 1990 creó su propia firma y presentó su primera colección de alta costura, con excelentes resultados. Ha presentado sus desfiles en lugares tan particulares como la Estación Central de Trenes de Atenas, y sus últimas colecciones están avaladas por el aplauso del público estadounidense en Nueva York.

VICTORIO & LUCCHINO / www.victorioylucchino.com

José Luis Medina del Corral, from Seville and José Víctor Rodríguez, from Cordoba, Spain, created Victorio & Lucchino in the late seventies. There are six elements that define their unmistakable style: color, lace, embellishment defined by fringing, flounce, brides with their own identity and the fusion of tradition of Southern Spain with cutting-edge fashion. Their proposals are shown each season at the Cibeles Madrid Fashion Week and have been presented on the runways of New York, Milan, Barcelona, Germany and Japan, among others.

José Luis Medina del Corral aus Sevilla und José Víctor Rodríguez aus Córdoba gründeten Ende der 70er Jahre Victorio & Lucchino. Ihr unverwechselbarer Stil wird durch sechs Elemente definiert: Farbe, Spitze, Fransenverzierungen, Volants, Brautkleider mit eigener Identität und einer Fusion aus Tradition und Avantgarde. Ihre Entwürfe werden jede Saison bei der Cibeles Madrid Fashion Week präsentiert und waren unter anderem auf den internationalen Laufstegen in New York, Mailand, Barcelona, Deutschland und Japan erfolgreich.

José Luis Medina del Corral, de Sevilla, y José Víctor Rodríguez, de Córdoba, crearon Victorio & Lucchino a finales de los setenta. Son seis los elementos que definen su estilo inconfundible: el color, el encaje, el ornamento marcado por el fleco, el volante, las novias con identidad propia y la fusión de la tradición del sur con la vanguardia. Sus propuestas se presentan cada temporada en la Cibeles Madrid Fashion Week y han recorrido las pasarelas de Nueva York, Milán, Barcelona, Alemania y Japón, entre otras.

VLADISLAV AKSENOV / www.vladislavaksenov.com

The Russian designer Vladislav Aksenov created his menswear company in 2007; shattering conceptions with his first collection, zero zero one, in Saint Petersburg Fashion Week, with a style that blends luxury and military style. The label has two lines: the first, Vladislav Aksenov, for serious and respectable people; the second line, Varan, is for those who prefer an unusual and daring temperament. In addition, Vladislav also devotes part of his creative energy to interior design.

Der russische Designer Vladislav Aksenov gründete sein Unternehmen für Herrenmode 2007 und überschritt mit seiner ersten Kollektion unter dem Titel zero zero one bei der Saint Petersburg Fashion Week mit seinem Stil aus Luxus- und Military-Elementen gleich mehrere Grenzen. Die erste, Vladislav Aksenov, zeichnet sich durch einen respektablen, seriösen Stil aus; die zweite Linie ist für Menschen, denen ungewöhnliche, mutige Mode gefällt. Außerdem widmet Vladislav Aksenov einen Teil seiner kreativen Energie dem Design von Interieurs.

El diseñador ruso Vladislav Aksenov creó su firma de moda masculina en 2007, rompiendo los esquemas con su primera colección, zero zero one, en la Saint Petersburg Fashion Week, con un estilo que mezcla el lujo y el estilo militar. La firma cuenta con dos líneas: la primera, Vladislav Aksenov, para gente seria y respetable; la segunda línea, Varan, es para aquellos a los que les gusta lo inusual y atrevido. Además, Vladislav también dedica parte de su energía creativa al diseño de interiores.

VRL COLLECTION / www.vrl-collection.jimdo.com

Born in Cadiz, Spain, Paco Varela is the fashion designer and stylist behind the firm VRL Collection, based in Madrid. After his experience working for the Portuguese designer Alexandra, he set up his own company. His collections have been presented in various editions of Pasarela Costello in Madrid, Jovens Criadores in Lisbon, South 36-32N in Cadiz, with romantic and elegant collections for men and women with a predominance of light and transparent fabrics.

Im spanischen Cádiz geboren, ist Paco Varela der Modedesigner und Stylist hinter dem Label VRL Collection mit Sitz in Madrid. Nach seiner Tätigkeit für die portugiesische Designerin Alexandra gründete er sein eigenes Unternehmen, dessen Kollektionen mehrfach auf der Modeschau Costella de Madrid, der Criadores de Lisboa und bei der South 36-32N in Cádiz gezeigt wurden. Seine Kollektionen für Damen und Herren sind romantisch und elegant und zeichnen sich durch leichte, transparente Stoffe aus.

Nacido en Cádiz (España), Paco Varela es el diseñador de moda y estilista que se encuentra detrás de la firma VRL Collection, con sede en Madrid. Después de su experiencia trabajando para la diseñadora portuguesa Alexandra, creó su propia firma, cuyas colecciones se han presentado en varias ediciones de la pasarela Costello de Madrid, en Jovens Criadores de Lisboa y en la South 36-32N de Cádiz, con colecciones para hombre y mujer románticas y elegantes, con predominio de tejidos ligeros y transparencias.